The Basic Basics
PRESSURE COOKER
COOKBOOK

The Basic Basics

PRESSURE COOKER COOKBOOK

Marguerite Patten

Grub Street • London

Published in 2010 by
Grub Street
4 Rainham Close
London
SW11 6SS

Email: food@grubstreet.co.uk
Web: www.grubstreet.co.uk

First published in Great Britain by William Collins Sons & Co in
1977 as *Marguerite Patten's Pressure Cookery*

A CIP catalogue record for this book is available from the British
Library

ISBN 978-1-906502-62-1

Printed and bound in Great Britain by
MPG Books Ltd, Bodmin, Cornwall

This book has been printed on FSC (Forest Stewardship Council)
paper

PUBLISHER'S NOTE

The publisher wishes to thank manufacturers Prestige, Tefal and
WMF for so generously supplying pressure cookers for testing and
for allowing the publisher to reproduce information from their
instruction manuals.

CONTENTS

INTRODUCTION   7

STARTERS   18

MAKING STOCKS AND SOUPS   24

COOKING FISH   51

COOKING MEAT, POULTRY AND GAME   67

COOKING VEGETABLES   109

COOKING RICE, PASTA AND CEREALS   119

PUDDINGS AND CAKES   124

MAKING PRESERVES   146

INDEX   157

INTRODUCTION

I was first involved with pressure cookers at a press launch in 1949 and so having enjoyed their benefits in my own home for over sixty years, I do appreciate the time and fuel they save in cooking.

Often I am asked just how I use the cooker. When I reply, I realize to what an extent I rely on it for so many cooking processes. You will find these described, with my own favourite pressure cooking recipes, in this book, but to give a brief indication of the versatility of a pressure cooker I list the main purposes below.

I hate wasting food of any kind, so bones, poultry and game carcasses are put into the cooker to produce a rich stock which gives the basis for interesting soups, stews and many savoury dishes.

Like many women today, I have a career as well as running my own home, and time is precious. It is a great relief to be able to produce an interesting main dish with beans, meat or poultry in a matter of minutes, not hours.

The British varieties of steamed pudding are famous, and deservedly so, for they are delicious and often very nutritious too. So why are they not made more often? I think it is because of the time needed to cook them and also the bother of filling up the pan under the steamer, and enduring the steam in the kitchen during the cooking process. You will find you not only save time in cooking the puddings if you use a pressure cooker, but you no longer have to worry about needing to replenish the pan with boiling water during cooking.

There are other important advantages. Rather elderly vegetables or cheaper cuts of meat, which might well be hard or tough, if cooked by conventional methods, can be made tender and full of flavour by this quicker method of cooking. You will notice I use the words 'full of flavour', for one of the pleasures of pressure cooking is to find you retain so much of the good taste of the vegetables, fruit, meat, etc.

There are certain dishes which often cause problems in cooking; among them I would list egg custards (both sweet and savoury). These need very careful attention to temperature and timing to ensure success. You will see that dishes based upon egg custards are cooked perfectly and simply in a matter of minutes.

Often people say that a pressure cooker must be a great boon to a large family; indeed it is, but it also enables a person living alone to cook a complete meal in the one pan, so saving both fuel and effort in washing up afterwards.

Most of us like to have a good store cupboard containing preserves of all kinds and most people today own a freezer. When making marmalades, jams, or preparing dishes for the freezer or for bottling, you will find your pressure cooker is invaluable.

I have stressed that I, like most people, hate wasting food, but I am sure you all agree with me that it is also important to save time and money. This you will do if you make full use of your pressure cooker. To produce a stew or soup in minutes, using one burner or hotplate only on a low heat, after bringing up to pressure, must be cheaper than using the same part of the cooker, or the oven, for several hours.

I think most families would say they require appetizing food at a price they can afford, and the kind of food which is easy to cook and which does them good.

This is why home cooking of good basic fresh ingredients forms a sound foundation for healthy eating. Over the years many scientific experiments have been carried out on the results of pressure cooking and it has been found that the food is not only good to eat, but retains the maximum of mineral salts and vitamins too, so pressure cooking can be described as a healthy form of cooking, as well as a speedy, fuel- and money-saving method.

Most women go out to work today, and they will find that so many recipes that were difficult to cook for the family in the evening, because of the prolonged cooking period, are now easily cooked within a short time. Planning well ahead means you can often pressure-cook extra vegetables, fruit, etc., for the next day.

People who live alone often say they 'cannot be bothered' to do much cooking. I hope they will look at pages 52, 106-108 and 121, for on these pages there are suggestions for complete meals in the pressure cooker.

Baby food may seem a great deal of trouble, but often the special dish required for the baby or small child can be placed in the cooker and prepared with the family meal. This is covered within the book.

There are times when we all want something rather special, maybe for a special celebration meal or when we are entertaining. I am a great believer in perfecting a basic recipe, then finding ways to adapt this, so that it becomes suitable for all occasions, but never monotonous. Many of the recipes have a 'Gourmet Touch' note at the end with recipe suggestions; these will enable you to shine as a sophisticated, as well as a wise and economical, cook.

I am confident you, and your family, will benefit as much as I have by using this method of cooking. I trust that the recipes and information in this book will be helpful.

Marguerite Patten

HOW THE COOKER WORKS

Although various models have their own particular features, the general principles are similar.

Until pressure is built up inside the cooker you have ordinary elegant utensils that look like saucepans. Indeed at times you will use the cooker just like an ordinary pan, e.g. when frying meat, vegetables, etc., for a stew; when thickening soups or stews at the end of cooking; after softening peel and fruit for marmalade, jams, etc.

Normally liquids boil at a temperature of 100°C (212°F). This temperature is controlled by atmospheric pressure and cannot increase, *no matter how long* boiling continues. If the atmospheric pressure can be increased, *then* the temperature at which liquids boil can be raised accordingly. This is the basic principle behind pressure cooking.

The ingredients, and liquid in which they are cooked, are enclosed in a safe, steam-proof vessel. This means the steam, which normally escapes into the atmosphere from an ordinary pan, is controlled and only allowed to escape under pressure. As you seal in steam, you then build up a higher pressure, which in turn produces a higher boiling point inside the cooker. This is the reason why foods are cooked so much more quickly and so efficiently.

Most modern pressure cookers have a choice of two pressures. This enables you to select the right temperature for various cooking processes and so achieve the best results. In all recipes in this book you will find the recommended pressure.

It is interesting to know exactly the temperature inside the cooker at the various pressures.

Pressure	Temperature
Atmospheric	Boiling point 100°C (212°F)
L (5 lb) –	Boiling point 108.5°C (228°F)
M (10 lb) –	Boiling point 115.3°C (239.8°F)
H (15 lb) –	Boiling point 122°C (252°F)

THE EFFECT OF ALTITUDE

The atmospheric pressure decreases the higher one gets above sea-level, and the boiling point of liquids decreases with it. A pressure cooker can compensate for this, but adjustments must then be made to

a) cooking times, or

b) pressures shown in the recipes in this book; e.g. over 600 metres (2000 feet) above sea-level, recipes at H(15 lb) pressure should be increased by ONE MINUTE for every 300 metres (1000 feet).

Recipes at M(10 lb) pressure should be cooked at H(15 lb) pressure and recipes at L(5 lb) pressure should be cooked at M(10 lb) pressure. When raising the pressure like this do not increase the cooking time.

PARTS OF A PRESSURE COOKER

The pan: Keep this clean (see page 13). When using the cooker for steamed puddings, etc., it is a good idea to put in lemon juice or vinegar to prevent the pan from discolouring (see page 125).

The lid: This is the cover for the pressure cooker. Clean carefully and check it is always locked in position, according to the manufacturer's instructions.

The gasket: This is the ring inside the cover and it seals the gap between the cover and the base and makes the pressure cooker steam-tight. Always clean carefully (see page 13).

The trivet: This enables food to be cooked above the minimum of liquid necessary, i.e. 280 ml (½ pt), in a pressure cooker. The trivet is placed with the rim downwards into the pan; recipes state if this is used.

The separator/steamer basket: You may have several separators or just one with a division. Most useful for keeping different foods apart (see pages 106-8).

Safety plug/valve: Should the vent become blocked, excess pressure builds up inside the cooker until the metal centre of the safety plug springs up and releases the excess of steam.

To avoid this: Never fill the complete cooker more than two-thirds full with solids, or the base of the cooker more than half full with liquids, and solids such as soup, milk puddings, etc.

To replace the metal centre of the safety plug allow all steam to go from the cooker, then remove the cover and place this upside-down and gently, but firmly, press the metal centre back into position. Make sure the centre vent is clear before continuing the cooking.

20 IMPORTANT SAFETY TIPS

• Read the operating manual of your particular model before attempting to cook with it.

• Do not allow anyone to use a pressure cooker before they have first read all the instructions for use.

• Do keep children away from the pressure cooker while it is being used.

• Before using a new pressure cooker for the first time wash the pan and lid in hot soapy water.

- Ensure that the lid is in place and locked before heating the cooker.
- Never use force to open up the lid.
- Never open it before all the pressure has subsided.
- Never bring the cooker up to pressure without adding liquid.
- Always provide a minimum of 280 ml (½ pt) of liquid.
- Never use oil or fat as the cooking liquid.
- Never fill the pressure cooker to more than ⅔ of its capacity. This includes the liquid you are adding.
- For foods that expand or froth during cooking, such as grains, beans, pulses, rice and dried vegetables, only fill the cooker half full including the liquid.
- Never use a pressure cooker to deep fry food in oil under pressure.
- Do not pressure cook dumplings.
- If you cook on gas do not allow the flame to lick up the sides of the pan; the outside of the pan will become discoloured and the handles may overheat.
- Never use your pressure cooker in the oven.
- Always handle the pressure cooker with extreme care especially if it contains hot liquid.
- To avoid damage to the pan do not allow the pressure cooker to boil dry.
- Always shake the pressure cooker before opening to release any pockets of steam trapped in the food, which may result in scalding.
- Each time you use your pressure cooker check that the safety devices, seals and valves are working properly.

STEP BY STEP TO PERFECT PRESSURE COOKING

Always follow the instructions given by the manufacturer regarding the particular model. There is an instruction book provided. If you have lost it call the manufacturer for a replacement.

1   Prepare the recipe.

2   Get the pressure cooker ready; check whether you will need the trivet and/or separator.

3   Pour the correct amount of water, or other liquid, into the pan;

the minimum quantity to use must be 280 ml (½pt). There are recipes where you brown the food in the open pan first, then add the liquid. Be sure to scrape up any browned pieces of food from the bottom of the pot to prevent them burning.

4   Add the ingredients to the cooker.

5   Put on the lid and make sure this is firmly locked, according to the manufacturer's instructions.

6   Place cooker over heat. Where cooking food with a high proportion of liquid, e.g. soups, milk puddings, etc., heat steadily. This is to prevent the liquid boiling up and blocking the vent or safety device. When cooking other foods use a high heat.

7   Bring to pressure. Continue heating over a high heat (or medium heat, see stage 6) until you hear a faint 'hiss' followed by a louder one as steam escapes, this indicates the pressure has been reached. Most modern pressure cookers have a round pressure indicator, with red or orange rings, which rises and the rings become visible. The time it takes to reach high pressure will depend on the type and quantity of ingredients in the cooker. For example soups which have a large amount of liquid could take up to 15 minutes.

8   Lower the heat to maintain the required pressure and start to time the pressure cooking. When recipes give the pressure cooking time, they mean the time from when the heat is lowered. You will soon get into the habit of careful timing, for this is important. This is no more difficult than checking the cooking speed in an ordinary pan.

9   At the end of the cooking period turn off the heat or remove the cooker to a cold hob. You will now need to reduce the pressure before removing the lid. How this is achieved is dependent upon the model of your pressure cooker and again you should refer to the manual of instructions. In general though to reduce pressure in most cookers either:

   a) reduce quickly by cold water release – stand the cooker in a metal sink or bowl of cold water or allow cold water to flow over the outside of the cooker. Make sure none runs over the safety plug or centre vent. Use this method for foods which you want to stop cooking immediately and are easy to overcook, such as vegetables and fish.

   b) reduce slowly by the natural release method – leave the cooker to cool naturally away from the heat of the hotplate or boiling ring. Use this method for foods where it is beneficial for them to continue cooking and will not overcook, such as soups, stews, root vegetables, pulses and grains.

   c) reduce normally by the automatic release method – activate the pressure release button according to the manufacturer's instructions.

10 Remove the food from the cooker and serve.

11 In some recipes such as stews, sauces, etc., you thicken the liquid before removing food from the cooker. Blend in the thickening, stir over a low to medium heat until smooth and of the correct consistency. Taste and adjust seasoning to your satisfaction, then serve.

LOOKING AFTER A PRESSURE COOKER

Washing up: Wash the pan after use with the same care and washing-up detergent you use to keep your ordinary pans clean. Rinse well in clean water and dry thoroughly before storing the cooker. *Never use soda as this could affect the aluminium.* Clean inside the cover well, and remove any food on the gasket, wash well in detergent solution, rinse and dry. Rinse the inside rim of the cover, then replace the gasket carefully. If the aluminium base of the cooker becomes discoloured or darkens, do not worry, remove the stain with soap pads, or simmer a strong solution of cream of tartar, vinegar or lemon rinds in water for 20 minutes. At the end of this time the metal will shine once again.

Centre vent: Always inspect this vent on the cover after cooking and cleaning; if it is blocked, clean under running hot water or with a pipe cleaner or skewer.

Coloured pressure cookers: Clean the inside as above, but wipe away any marks on the outside as soon as they appear. Use a soft cloth for this purpose, as abrasive scouring pads or cleaning powders can mark the coloured surface.

Non-stick models: These cookers have a Teflon (the Du Pont registered trade mark) finish and need extra care both in use and in cleaning. Before using Teflon models for the first time wash the coated surface with detergent solution, using a soft cloth. Condition the inside surface by wiping with a little cooking oil on a soft paper tissue or towel. Repeat occasionally. Avoid the use of electric or metal beaters or sharp knives, etc., in the pan. It is better to use wooden spatulas or spoons whenever possible.

If frying in the cooker use a medium heat only, as excessive heating of fat is not good for the surface. After use wash the cooker as above. You can use nylon, plastic or rubber scourers to remove marks but not abrasive scouring pads.

Storage of the pressure cooker: Make sure the cooker is dry before you put it away: this prevents pitting of the aluminium (formation of tiny pin-sized holes). When you are not using the cooker leave it open, with the lid reversed to allow air circulation and so prevent any smell of mustiness. Do not stand other metal pans on the base or lid, for it is important that the rim is not damaged. If it is an old style model store the weights carefully beside the cooker, so they are readily available.

PRESSURE COOKERS AND FREEZING

You will find your pressure cooker invaluable for preparing foods for the freezer. For example, you can:

a)   Prepare larger quantities of soups, stews, sauces, cooked fruit, etc., eat and enjoy some of the food for a meal the day it is cooked, and freeze the remainder for future occasions.

b)   Use the pressure cooker for 'blanching' vegetables ready for freezing (see page 150).

c)   Prepare fruit purées, citrus peel and pulp ready to make jam or marmalade at a convenient time; this is described on page 146.

One of the great advantages of a freezer is to be able to take frozen vegetables, stews, puddings, etc., from the freezer then cook, or heat, for a speedy meal. The pressure cooker can reduce the cooking or heating time and so combine with your freezer to give you even greater convenience.

You will find more details in each chapter heading.

BECOME AN EXPERT

The previous pages, and the instructions supplied by the manufacturer, will quickly enable you to become familiar with your particular pressure cooker. Within a very short time I have no doubt you will be using it for many forms of cooking and wondering how you ever managed without it. The recipes you use will not vary a great deal from those you have followed in the past, except that you will no longer cook in hours but often in only minutes.

You will need to plan meal preparation a little differently. Cooking times are so short in the pressure cooker that I put serving plates to warm before I begin cooking, and then set the table as the stew or other dish is cooking. I have mentioned earlier that careful timing of the cooking period is important, do not let this worry you. At first, cook for a minute or so less time than that given in the recipe, particularly for meat dishes. The recipes have all been carefully tested and timed, but you may well chop the food into slightly smaller pieces than I have done, or the meat you use may be a little more tender. It is so easy to replace the cover, if you decide the food is not quite ready, bring up to pressure again and complete the cooking. When you first embark on a particular form of cooking, e.g. pot roasting or making a steamed pudding, I would suggest you read the chapter heading before actually making up the dish; this will outline the most important factors for that type of dish.

ADAPTING YOUR FAVOURITE RECIPES FOR THE PRESSURE COOKER

1   Reduce the liquid in the recipe so that it does not exceed the maximum fill of your cooker.

2   The minimum quantity of liquid (280 ml/½ pt) is all that is required in many recipes since there is almost no evaporation during cooking. But check the required minimum and maximum levels of your particular model.

3   Use 280 ml /½ pt of liquid for the first 15 minutes of cooking, for each additional 15 minutes or part of 15 minutes add a further 140 ml/¼ pt of liquid. So for example 30 minutes cooking will require 420 ml/¾ pt of liquid. This is only a general guide and grains and pulses and steamed puddings may require more water.

4   Calculate cooking times by comparing your recipe to another one in this book. So take your favourite soup recipe and compare to another similar one here.

5   To avoid over cooking if you are trying out your own recipes in the pressure cooker, release the pressure after the minimum recommended cooking time. You can always finish off the cooking with the pan open. However if it is very undercooked and there is still liquid in the pan, lock the lid back in place and bring the cooker back up to pressure.

6   For stewing or braising meat as a general rule allow 20 minutes per 450 g/1 lb of meat and use 250 ml/9 fl oz and then allow 125 ml/4 fl oz for each additional 450 g/1 lb.

7   For steam-roasting poultry, brown in oil first and then place on the trivet and add 250 ml/9 fl oz liquid. Cook for 5 minutes per 450 g/1 lb for unstuffed and 8 minutes per 450 g/1 lb for stuffed poultry.

BABY FOODS

Glass feeding bottles can be sterilized in a pressure cooker. It is essential that the bottles and teats used for feeding the baby are sterilized with the greatest of care. If you do this under pressure you ensure that harmful bacteria are quickly and successfully destroyed. Wash and rinse the used bottles and teats very carefully, rub a little salt into the teat to remove any milk left round the hole.

Put the trivet and 280 ml (½ pt) water into the cooker. Stand the washed bottles on this. Place the teats in a covered jar and stand on the trivet. Place the cover on the cooker and bring to M/10 lb/second ring pressure gradually. Lower the heat and sterilize for 5 minutes. Allow pressure to drop at room temperature.

If you are not using the cooker, the bottles can be left in with the lid and weight in position.

As the baby begins to need more solid foods make use of the cooker to cook small portions of fish, liver, chicken and vegetables. Put these into a small container, so they are cooked apart from the family meal, then sieve or purée. The timing for all groups of foods will be found in the pages that follow.

When serving fruit purées (page 142) or egg custard (page 134) take care not to sweeten too much, as modern dieticians do not advocate the use of much sugar in baby foods.

PET FOOD

You can feed cats and dogs efficiently and economically using cheaper meats, such as ox liver, which take a very long time to cook by the usual methods. You will find the pressure cooker excellent for this purpose. The timing for meats and fish will be found in the appropriate chapters of this book.

A NOTE ON HERBS

Mention is made of **bouquet garni** in a number of recipes. Choose parsley (the stalks give most flavour), chives, thyme (lemon or English), a very little sage, plus rosemary or tarragon or basil according to the particular dish. To make bouquet garni: tie chosen herbs in a bunch with thread, or place in a muslin bag, and tie. Remove the herbs before serving the dish unless the sauce or soup is sieved or emulsified in a blender.

METRICATION

Both metric and imperial measures are given in this book. One golden rule is to follow *either* the metric measures *or* the imperial ones, for that way you keep everything in proportion. It is not wise to 'dodge' from column to column.

WEIGHTS
The accurate conversion is:

28.35 g equals 1 oz
1 kg equals 2.2 lb.

It has been decided to take 25 g as 1 oz; when you get to larger quantities, i.e. above 6 oz, you need to step up the amount of grams to give similar quantities of food.

e.g. 6 x 25 equals 150 g, which is appreciably less than 6 oz, so I call 6 oz – 170 g which gives the same quantity as 6 oz. (If your scales register in units of 25, weigh very slightly below 175 g.) In most cases in this book 4 oz is given as 100 g, but in a pudding, when I want the measurements to be exact, I remind you to be a little more generous with flour, etc., by weighing 110 g or a generous 100 g. Often 0.5 kg is shown as 1 lb; this is when you need not be bothered about slight differences between metric and imperial. Where I think it is important to be accurate I call 1 lb – 450 g.

LIQUIDS
The measure here is a litre (l); 1 litre equals 1.75 pints (pt). Where small quantities are required, we use millilitres (ml) in this book, elsewhere you may see decilitres (dl). 142 ml (or 1.5 dl) is the equivalent of ¼ pint. Although often 125 ml is given as the equivalent of ¼ pt, I feel that is a little low for cooking, so I give 140 ml. Where the quantity of liquid does not need to be too exact I often talk about a generous ½ l as 1 pint.

STARTERS

The following pâtés, and similar recipes, are ideal for a starter or a light lunch. The more substantial terrines on page 93-94 are equally suitable for a light main dish, served with salad and crusty fresh bread. Some of the fish or vegetable dishes in this book can be adapted as a first course. Most of the recipes are will serve 4 people as a main course. You could serve smaller portions to 6–8 people, if you choose to make them as a starter, from exactly the same quantities.

COOKING PÂTÉS IN A PRESSURE COOKER

The secret of cooking a pâté in the oven is to keep it moist. This is done by standing the tin or dish in a bain-marie, i.e. a container of water. The pressure cooker is an ideal means of cooking pâtés, as the steam inside the cooker prevents the mixture from becoming dry round the sides, in the same way as a bain-marie. The pâté is cooked in a much shorter time than usual. If you want to cook one of your favourite pâtés in a pressure cooker then reduce the amount of liquid in your recipe by one-third. The reason for this is there is more evaporation in the oven than in a pressure cooker.

FREEZING PÂTÉS
If you make a larger amount of pâté in your pressure cooker, or prepare it in advance for a dinner party, then it can be frozen for a period of 4–6 weeks. After this time it tends to become dry and lose flavour and colour. Cover the pâté well before freezing.

To serve: allow to defrost overnight in the refrigerator;

USING A BLENDER
A blender saves time in pounding the liver, etc., in a pâté or rillettes. If making the Luxury Pâté (see page 21), proceed to the end of stage 5, then put the liver, onion, cream and liquid into the blender, liquidise until smooth, remove from the goblet, add the diced gherkins and tongue. For a perfectly smooth pâté liquidise the gherkins and tongue with the other ingredients.
  When making the rillettes put the cooked giblet meat (free from

bones), the cooked onion, butter and all the other ingredients into the goblet and liquidise.

KIPPER PÂTÉ

This is an economical and quickly made pâté. Buy kipper fillets, rather than kippers, to save time in removing bones. Cook the kipper fillets for 1–2 minutes at H/15 lb pressure (see page 59). Flake the fish while hot and put the flesh into a basin. To each 4 kipper fillets blend in 50 g (5 oz) melted butter, 1 crushed clove garlic, 1 tablespoon lemon juice, a pinch grated nutmeg and black pepper. Stir well to obtain a smooth mixture. Put into four small containers, top with a little melted butter and allow to cool. Serve with hot toast and butter.

TO VARY:

Bloaters can be used instead, allow 4–5 minutes cooking time, at H/15 lb pressure.

FAMILY LIVER PÂTÉ

Serves 6–8
Pressure cooking time 20 mins

0.5 kg (1 lb) pig's liver
225 g (8 oz) fat bacon or belly of pork
140 ml (¼ pt) double cream
2 tablespoons stock
2 eggs
salt and pepper

TO COVER:
50 g (2 oz) butter (optional)

1　Put the liver and bacon or pork through a mincer; either use the coarse blade, or mince the meats once or twice with the fine blades for a smooth pâté.

2　Mix with the other ingredients, season well.

3　Put into a 1litre (1¾-pt) basin or soufflé dish, do not fill more than two-thirds; cover with a double thickness of buttered grease-proof paper or foil.

4　Put the trivet into the cooker and add 420 ml (¾ pt) water.

5 Stand the container on the trivet, fix the cover, bring to H/15 lb pressure.

6 Lower the heat and cook for 20 minutes, allow the pressure to drop at room temperature.

7 Take the container out of the cooker, remove the damp cover, put on a dry piece of greased greaseproof paper or foil.

8 If you place a light weight on the pâté as it cools it will have a better texture for slicing.

9 Serve with hot toast and butter.

10 You can store the pâté in the refrigerator for several days or in the freezer for 4–6 weeks, in which case melt the butter, pour over the pâté and allow it to set. Garnish with lemon and lettuce, if desired.

TO VARY:
Add either
    a)   little grated lemon rind and juice or
    b)   1 tablespoon chopped fresh herbs (sage, lemon thyme, parsley and tarragon) or
    c)   a good pinch ground nutmeg, cinnamon and powdered mace.

Use a thick white sauce made with 25 g (1 oz) butter, 25 g (1 oz) flour and 140 ml (¼ pt) milk instead of the double cream.

Fry 1 finely chopped onion and/or 1–2 chopped garlic cloves in 25 g (1 oz) butter, add to liver, etc.

Gourmet Touch: Use sherry or brandy in place of stock.

TARAMASALATA

Although some recipes for this smoked cod's roe pâté are made without cooking, this particular recipe produces a less strong flavour.

Serves 6–8
Pressure cooking time 5 mins

0.5 kg (1 lb) smoked cod's roe
1–2 cloves garlic
75 g (3 oz) butter
3 tablespoons soft white breadcrumbs
2 tablespoons double cream
½ tablespoon lemon juice
Shake of pepper

---

1 Remove all the skin from the roe.

2 Peel and crush the garlic.

3 Cream the butter then blend with the other ingredients.

4 Continue as in Family Liver Pâté, stages 3–10, but allow only 5 minutes cooking at H/15 lb pressure.

TO VARY:

Seafood Pâté: An excellent pâté is made by using half smoked cod's roe and half minced or pounded raw white fish. This will appeal to people who find the pâté with all smoked roe a little too definite in flavour. Cook in the same way as the pâté on page 19 for 5 minutes only at H/15 lb pressure.

Gourmet Touch: Instead of 2 tablespoons cream, use 1 tablespoon dry sherry and 1 tablespoon cream.

Créme à la Grecque: This is a slightly more economical recipe and one that gives a milder flavour than the uncooked version of this classic pâté. Follow directions for Taramasalata, page 20, but omit cream and add 2 tablespoons sieved fresh tomato pulp instead. Cook as Taramasalata. Serve with black olives.

Salmon Pâté: Use raw fresh salmon or half fresh salmon and half uncooked white fish instead of the smoked cod's roe. Put the fish through a mincer or pound until very smooth then follow directions for Taramasalata, seasoning with salt and pepper. Bind with an egg then cook as Taramasalata, above.

LUXURY PÂTÉ

Serves 4
Pressure cooking time 3 mins

---

1 small onion
50 g (2 oz) butter
225 g (8 oz) chicken livers or calves' liver
Salt and pepper
4 tablespoons double cream
2 tablespoons brandy or sherry or stock
2 gherkins
50 g (2 oz) cooked tongue

---

1   Peel and grate the onion or chop very finely.

2   Melt the butter and blend with the onion.

3   Wash, dry and season the liver, put into a small tin and add the butter and onion, cover with greased greaseproof paper.

4   Place the trivet in the pressure cooker, add 280 ml (½ pt) water, then stand the tin on the trivet.

5   Fix the cover, bring up to H/15 lb pressure, then cook for 3 minutes for chicken livers or thinly sliced calves' liver, but slightly longer if thickly sliced.

6   Reduce the pressure under cold water, lift out the liver and pound with the onion and butter until smooth. Cool, then blend with the cream and brandy, sherry or stock.

7   Dice the gherkins and tongue and stir into the pâté.

8   Cover the dish with foil, so the pâté does not dry on top, or cover the pâté with melted butter, and store for at least 24 hours in the refrigerator before serving.

9   Serve with hot toast and butter.

TO VARY:

To give a stronger flavour add garlic salt or 1–2 crushed garlic cloves to the butter and onion.

A very subtle flavour is given to a pâté if cream cheese is used instead of the double cream. Blend 50–75 g (2–3 oz) cream cheese (amount depends entirely upon personal taste) into the cold liver mixture, proceed as above.

Gourmet Touch: Serve the pâté with Cumberland Sauce (see page 102).

RILLETTES

This is an adaptation of the well-known French spread. It is an ideal way of using all the meat from the giblets of turkey, chicken, etc., and having a good flavoured stock to serve with roast poultry.

1   Put the well-washed giblets into the pressure cooker with 420 ml (¾ pt) water, salt and pepper to taste.

2   Fix the cover, bring up to H/15 lb pressure and cook chicken or duckling giblets for 10 minutes, but allow 15 minutes for the giblets of turkey, goose and older boiling fowl.

3   Reduce the pressure under cold water, lift out the giblets and pull

all the meat from the neck, and finely chop the heart, liver etc.

4   Grate 1 small onion and toss in 25–50 g (1–2 oz) butter until soft then add to the giblet meat.

5   Pound the meat and onion mixture until smooth then mix with the cream, etc., as in the Luxury Pâté (page 21). The giblet meat takes the place of the liver. The tongue can be omitted.

6   Serve with hot toast and butter.

MAKING STOCKS AND SOUPS

Many years ago a stock pot was an essential part of any good cook's kitchen. The bones were kept simmering in liquid for many hours, producing a rich stock which added a delicious flavour to soups, sauces, stews and gravies. We now realize this was a far from perfect way to make the stock, and greatly appreciate the speed and efficiency of a pressure cooker. The stock produced from bones in a pressure cooker is richer than any made in an ordinary saucepan or stock pot.

The recipes for making stocks are given on pages 25-28.

One of the most satisfying of all dishes is a bowl of really good soup, generally steaming hot, but sometimes served as a cool and refreshing start to a meal.

It gives one a splendid feeling to know that from a pressure cooker you can produce enough soup for all the family, often in a matter of minutes. And good soup can be made from a few vegetables, or meat left on the bones, or flesh from the carcass of game or poultry.

There are certain points to remember when making a stock or soup:

Capacity: Do not have the pan more than half full. If you want to make a large quantity of soup, you can reduce the liquid slightly so that the pan is not overfull, then add extra liquid when the soup is cooked to bring to the correct consistency.

Trivet: Do not use the trivet when making stock or soup; you want the ingredients to be cooked in the liquid.

Pressure: Bring up to H/15 lb pressure on a medium heat and allow the pressure to drop at room temperature.

Liquid: You will notice less liquid is given in most soup recipes than when cooking in a saucepan; this is because there is no evaporation when cooking in a pressure cooker.

Seasoning: As the ingredients cooked in the pressure cooker retain the maximum of their natural flavour, be sparing with salt, etc., when making stock and soups. Adjust seasoning at the end of the cooking time.

Reducing pressure: When making stocks or soups allow the pressure to drop steadily at room temperature; do not cool with cold water.

FREEZING STOCK AND SOUPS

If making stock or soups specifically to freeze, reduce the liquid to give a more concentrated mixture that will take up less room in the freezer. Cook by pressure, cool, remove the top layer of fat then pack and freeze. It is advisable to thicken soups when reheating after freezing, and also to add any cream or milk together with extra seasoning and wine, as they lose a little potency in freezing. Rice and pasta tend to become over-soft in a soup during freezing so they are better cooked in the soup when it is reheated.

To reheat the cooked soup: Put about 280 ml (½pt) stock or water into the open pan, plus any extra required by the recipe. Add the block of soup, heat gently for 2–3 minutes, then break up the block into small pieces. Fix the cover and bring steadily to H/15 lb pressure, then allow pressure to drop. Taste the soup, thicken if necessary, add any extra ingredients and seasoning and continue cooking or heating according to the individual recipe.

PRESENTATION OF SOUPS

Soups need interesting garnishes, preferably those which make a pleasing contrast in colour and texture. Chopped herbs, such as parsley, chives, mint, tarragon, look cool on brightly coloured or pale soups. Yogurt or cream or soured cream are excellent garnishes on both hot and cold soups.

Paprika gives colour, without adding too definite a flavour, to pale coloured soups.

Fried or toasted croutons are particularly good with vegetable soups. To make croutons, either dice sliced bread, fry in hot butter or oil, then drain; or toast bread and then dice. Put on top of the soup at the last minute, so that the soup does not make them soft.

STOCKS

You can use almost any bones to make stock. They can be from cooked meat or they can be fresh uncooked bones. Various bones can be mixed, unless you want a really white stock, but ham, game bird or bones from game such as venison tend to dominate other flavours, so are better used alone.

Vegetables add flavour to stock, but cause it to spoil more readily. *Always* store stock in the refrigerator or in the freezer. A pressure cooker enables you to make richer stocks that will give flavour to so many dishes. Here are the definitions of various types of stock:

Brown Stock: Made ideally from beef bones, shin is excellent, and so is a marrow bone which produces a rich stock and plenty of fat. Game bones give a good brown stock with a definite flavour and colour. Lamb and mutton stock is less adaptable than beef stock, but good in recipes such as Mulligatawny soup, page 46. If using vegetables choose a selection of root, not green, vegetables, plus celery and herbs such as thyme, marjoram and parsley. Season well. To make a browner stock, fry the vegetables in oil, dripping or butter in the open pressure cooker first. Bones from roasted joints give a darker stock than fresh bones or those from boiled meat.

Fish Stock: When the fish is cooked in liquid in the cooker it gives an excellently flavoured stock to add to sauces, but if you require a fish stock:

Put the bones and skin of fish into the pressure cooker with a strip of lemon rind, a bay leaf, bouquet garni (see page 16), then cover with water or water with a tablespoon lemon juice or white wine vinegar or 2–3 tablespoons white wine. Fix the cover, bring to H/15 lb ; cook for only 5 minutes. Strain and use.

Ham Stock: Use the bones from ham or boiled bacon. Ideal for many soups, particularly the pulses, page 37, and in dishes where a distinct flavour of bacon is an improvement. Use mixed root vegetables, marjoram and parsley and pepper only to season.

White Stock: Use veal bones for a perfect white stock and white vegetables, i.e. onion and celery, to flavour. Add a bay leaf, lemon thyme and lemon rind to flavour. Season lightly. Ideal for delicately flavoured soups and dishes.

Poultry Stock: The bones from the carcass of chicken and turkey can be used for a mild-flavoured stock. If you add the giblets, skin and inside of the body you darken the stock; flavour as White Stock, above. Duck and goose stock are darker and richer with a lot of fat; flavour with sage and a little orange rind.

Vegetable Stock: Excellent for vegetarian dishes. Use a selection of vegetables and herbs. To darken the stock, fry the sliced vegetables in hot oil or butter in the open pressure cooker first.

TO MAKE STOCK

Vegetables, bones, etc.

1   If frying vegetables, cook until golden in the open pressure cooker.

2   Break or crush the bones, for the smaller the pieces the more flavour is extracted.

3 Put the bones into the pressure cooker with almost enough water to cover, but make certain you have not more than half-filled the cooker.

4 Add the vegetables (unless these are first fried – see stage 1), then the herbs. As the stock is being strained, the herbs need not be tied in a bunch or in muslin as described in bouquet garni, page 16.

5 Fix the lid, bring steadily to H/15 lb pressure, and cook for the following times if possible: for a really rich stock, which can be diluted – to 2 hours; for a stock that can be used undiluted – from 30 minutes, if using bones from cooked meat, to 45 minutes for fresh bones.

6 Allow pressure to drop, then remove the cover and strain the stock. Allow to cool.

7 Lift the fat from the top of the stock. This can be used for frying. Hard fat from marrow bones can be clarified (see page 98) and used for pastry making.

CLEAR SOUPS

The following recipes are based upon the stocks on the previous page or the classic consommés given below. Consommé could be called the 'caviare' of stock, for the flavour is so rich that it needs little extra added to make a first-class soup.

BEEF CONSOMMÉ

Serves 4–6
Pressure cooking time 30 mins

---

340 g (12 oz) shin beef
1 litre (1¾ pt) brown stock, see page 25
1 onion
1 carrot
1 bay leaf
Little sherry (optional)

---

1 Cut the meat into small pieces.

2 Put into the pressure cooker with the rest of the ingredients, except the sherry.

3 Fix the cover, bring steadily to H/15 lb pressure, and then cook for 30 minutes.

4 Allow the pressure to drop, remove the cover.

5 Strain the soup most carefully. If you want it very clear, strain through several thicknesses of muslin or simmer 1–2 lightly whisked egg whites in the soup for a few minutes after stage 4, these pick up any tiny particles of meat, etc., then strain through muslin.

6 Add the sherry if desired and serve hot.

TO VARY:

Chicken Consommé: Use chicken stock instead of beef and a little diced raw chicken or veal for more flavour. Pieces of game, lamb, veal can be added to brown or white stock and cooked as above to produce other consommés, all of which can be garnished or served as below.

Consommé Indienne: Make the consommé, meanwhile fry a finely chopped onion in 25 g (1 oz) butter with 2 teaspoons curry powder. Add to the hot, strained consommé and heat in the open cooker for 1 minute.

Jellied Consommé: Make and strain the consommé. Measure the liquid and to each generous ½ litre (1 pt) add 1½ teaspoons gelatine, softened in 2 tablespoons sherry or port. Stir until dissolved in the hot soup, allow to cool and set lightly. Whisk sharply and serve in cold soup cups.

If you make the original stock (see page 26) with veal bones or half veal and half beef bones, then there will be sufficient natural gelatine in the stock to set lightly.

Jellied Tomato Consommé: Add a little fresh tomato purée to the consommé.

Iced Consommé: Make the consommé. Cool then freeze very lightly. Put into chilled soup cups and garnish with lemon wedges.

Danish Chicken Soup: Make the chicken stock on page 26, strain and return to the pressure cooker. To each 1litre (1¾ pt) stock add about 100 g (4 oz) neatly diced cooked chicken and about 225 g (8 oz) diced root vegetables. Fix the cover, bring to H/15 lb pressure and cook for just 1 minute, allow pressure to drop and remove the cover. Make tiny dumplings, as in the recipe on page 100, cook them in the liquid. Serve with finely chopped parsley to garnish,

Tomato Consommé: Make a white or poultry stock as on page 26, then strain. To each generous ½ litre (1 pt) allow 280 ml (½pt) tomato juice, 1 very finely chopped onion, 2–3 finely chopped sticks celery. Put the ingredients into the pressure cooker, fix the cover. Bring to H/15 lb pressure, cook for 2 minutes, then allow pressure to drop and remove the cover. Top with chopped basil and/or parsley.

Consommé Julienne: Make the basic consommé then add match-sticks of raw vegetable. Bring up to pressure and cook for 1 minute.

Consommé Jardinière: Use finely diced vegetables instead of the matchsticks in the recipe immediately above, cook in the same way.

VEGETABLE SOUPS

Most vegetables make excellent soups, either by themselves, or blended with other vegetables such as onion.

In many recipes it states 'white stock or water'. Naturally the stock will give a more savoury flavour to the soup, and white stock is a better choice than brown stock in most vegetable soup recipes, since it does not affect the colour or flavour of the vegetables. Do not imagine you cannot make a good vegetable soup if you have no stock available; the vegetables retain so much flavour when cooked under pressure that the soup will be very pleasant.

Herbs, such as parsley, chives, garlic, thyme, basil, etc., all add interest to vegetable soups.

In many recipes the vegetables are chopped. There is no need to take time chopping them finely when the soup is to be sieved, for they become so tender in the pressure cooker that sieving or liquidising in a blender is much easier than usual. Often you can beat the vegetables with a wooden spoon and they become a smooth purée. If time is precious the vegetables can be put in the cooker without chopping; allow 3–4 minutes longer cooking time, for whole onions, carrots, etc. You can mash whole vegetables with a potato masher to make a purée soup.

BORTSCH

This is a classic soup from Russia. There are many variations, but this particular recipe is equally good hot or cold.

Serves 4–6
Pressure cooking time 20 mins

1 large raw beetroot
2 tomatoes
2 medium potatoes
1 medium carrot
1 onion

225 g (8 oz) cabbage
25 g (1 oz) beef dripping or fat
Scant 1litre (1½ pt) brown or white stock or water
Salt and pepper
Bouquet garni (see page 16) or pinch mixed herbs
1–2 bay leaves

TO GARNISH:
parsley, yogurt or soured cream

---

1   Wash, peel, dice or grate the beetroot.

2   Peel and dice or grate the other vegetables, except the cabbage which should be shredded.

3   Melt the dripping or fat in the pan and fry the beetroot for 5 minutes.

4   Add the other vegetables with the stock or water, salt and pepper, herbs and bay leaves.

5   Put on the cover, bring steadily to H/15 lb pressure.

6   Lower the heat and cook for 20 minutes.

7   Allow the pressure to drop then remove the cover.

8   Serve topped with parsley. Add the yogurt or soured cream just before serving.

TO VARY:

Cold Bortsch: Follow basic recipe, but omit the cabbage. Chill and top with parsley and the yogurt or soured cream.

Bortsch with Cooked Beetroot: Follow basic recipe but use 1½ large cooked beetroot and allow 8 minutes pressure cooking.

Gourmet Touch: **Jellied Bortsch:** Follow basic recipe, omit cabbage. When cooked, sieve or liquidise, measure the purée. To each 560 ml (1pt) allow 1½ level teaspoons gelatine. Soften gelatine in 2 tablespoons cold stock or water, dissolve in the hot soup. Allow to set lightly, whisk slightly. Spoon into soup cups, top with yogurt or soured cream.

ARTICHOKE SOUP

This is a good soup from a starchy vegetable. The proportions could be used as a basis for other soups, such as potato, on page 32.

Serves 4–6
Pressure cooking time 10 mins

---

750 g (1½ lb) Jerusalem artichokes
2 teaspoons vinegar or lemon juice
420 ml (¾ pt) white stock or water
Salt and pepper
25 g (1 oz) flour
280 ml (½ pt) milk
25 g (1 oz) butter or margarine

TO GARNISH:
paprika, chopped parsley

---

1   Wash and peel the artichokes, halve if large. Keep in cold water with 1 teaspoon vinegar or lemon juice; drain.

2   Put into the pressure cooker with the stock or water, remaining teaspoon vinegar or lemon juice (this helps keep them white), a little salt and pepper.

3   Fix the cover and bring steadily to H/15 lb pressure.

4   Lower the heat, cook for 10 minutes.

5   Allow pressure to drop, remove cover.

6   Blend the flour with the milk.

7   Sieve or mash the artichokes or liquidise with the liquid and return to the pan, together with the milk mixture.

8   Bring the soup to the boil.

9   Add the butter or margarine and any extra seasoning required and cook for 2–3 minutes, stirring all the time until smooth. Serve topped with paprika and parsley.

TO VARY:

If the artichokes are small, scrub but do not peel; use rather less than 450 g (1 lb).

Use 340 g (12 oz) artichokes; add 2 large chopped onions and 2 large skinned, chopped tomatoes at stage 2.

Gourmet Touch: **Artichoke Cream:** Use only 140 ml (¼pt) milk at stage 6, continue to stage 9. Blend 2 egg yolks with 1 tablespoon dry sherry, 140 ml (¼ pt) single cream, whisk into the hot, but not boiling, milk and heat gently.

BASED UPON ARTICHOKE SOUP

The soups below are cooked in the same time as the Artichoke Soup, unless stated to the contrary.

Celeriac Soup: The delicious celery root makes an excellent soup. Use the same quantity of celeriac as artichokes in any of the recipes or variations above. Celeriac discolours easily, so follow steps in stage 1, on page 31.

Celery Soup: Use a good-sized head of celery instead of artichokes. Follow stages of basic recipe, but omit vinegar or lemon juice. Celery does not contain as much starch as artichokes, so you may need to increase the amount of flour slightly to give the desired consistency.

Celery and Almond Soup: Use the same amount of flour as in the recipe, above, and follow the same stages, but add 25 g (1 oz) ground almonds with the flour at stage 6. Top the soup with flaked almonds just before serving.

Potato Soup: One of the best flavoured soups when you have a good white stock. Use almost the same amount of potatoes as the artichokes in the basic recipe, page 31, but add 1–2 chopped onions or the white part of 1–2 leeks. Follow the basic recipe or any of the variations, but omit the vinegar or lemon juice. The pressure cooking time can be reduced to 8 minutes. Always be generous with the amount of butter in a potato soup. Stir an extra 25 g (1 oz) butter into the soup at stage 9.

Potato and Carrot Soup: Use half potatoes and half carrots to give the same weight as the artichokes in the recipe on page 31. Follow the basic recipe, or any of the variations. A little vinegar or lemon juice could be used at stage 2 to give a pleasant 'bite'.

CARROT SOUP

This is a typical, simple purée of an economical vegetable. Use the same recipe for turnips or other vegetables, adding various herbs to flavour.

Serves 4–6
Pressure cooking time 4–8 mins

450 g (1 lb) old carrots or 340 g (12 oz) young carrots
1 small onion
25 g (1 oz) butter (or some oil)
Bouquet garni (see page 16) or pinch mixed dried herbs
Scant 1litre (1½ pt) white stock or water
Salt and pepper

TO GARNISH:

watercress or parsley

1   Peel and chop large old carrots; scrub young carrots. Peel and chop the onion.

2   Melt the butter or heat the oil in the bottom of the cooker and fry the onion, taking care it does not discolour.

3   Add the carrots and the other ingredients.

4   Put on the cover, bring to H/15 lb pressure.

5   Lower the heat; allow 4 minutes for diced carrots, up to 8 minutes for whole young carrots.

6   Allow pressure to drop.

7   Rub the carrots through a sieve or liquidise with the liquid to give a thick purée.

8   Return to the cooker and reheat, add a little extra liquid (milk, stock or water) if too thick.

9   Serve garnished with small sprigs of watercress or parsley.

Gourmet Touch: **German Carrot Soup**: Prepare soup as in basic recipe, but use only generous ½ litre (1 pt) stock or water. After stage 7 blend purée with a white sauce made with 25 g (1 oz) butter, 25 g (1 oz) flour and 280 ml (½ pt) milk. Heat. Blend 2 egg yolks, 140 ml (¼ pt) single cream, a good pinch cayenne pepper. Whisk into the hot, but not boiling, soup, heat gently. Cook 100 g (4 oz) noodles, add to the soup just before serving.

BASED ON CARROT SOUP

The soups below are all made in a similar way to the carrot soup above. The vegetables produce a thick well-flavoured purée.

Vegetable Soup: Use a mixture of vegetables, e.g. carrots, a turnip, celery, 1 or 2 tomatoes, an extra onion, a potato, etc., instead of all carrots, and follow the recipe, above. This soup can be made with white stock, but it has a very good flavour if a brown or bacon stock is used instead.

Cream of Vegetable Soup: Use a mixture of vegetables as suggested above, but follow the method for the German Carrot Soup, omitting the noodles. If you want a more economical soup then omit the egg yolks and most of the cream and increase the amount of milk when making the sauce.

Vichyssoise Soup: This delicious soup – one of the most popular cold soups – is equally good when served hot. You need a first-class white stock. Use 6 medium leeks (the white part with a very little green stem) instead of the carrots in the recipe, above, plus 2–3 medium-sized old potatoes. The onion can be omitted if you intend serving the soup cold, but you will need 1 or 2 onions for a more robust flavour which is better in a hot soup. Choose a little parsley rather than mixed herbs to flavour. Follow the directions for the carrot soup, page 32, allowing 8 minutes pressure cooking time. Sieve or liquidise as in stage 7.

If serving the soup hot, then return to the pan and heat with a little cream or milk. If serving the soup cold, chill and dilute with cream, or cream and a little white wine.

Top the soup with chopped parsley and chopped chives before serving.

Green Vichyssoise: Use only 3 leeks and 170–225 g (6–8 oz) shelled peas instead of the rest of the leeks. This is particularly good served cold.

ONION SOUP

Serves 4–6
Pressure cooking time 3 mins

---

750 g (1½ lb) onions
50 g (2 oz) butter
Scant 1litre (1¾ pt) brown stock
Salt and pepper
Slices of toast or French bread
25–50 g (1–2 oz) grated cheese, such as Cheddar, Gruyère or Parmesan

---

1 Peel the onions and cut into thin rings; divide large rings into quarters.

2 Melt the butter in the cooker.

3 Fry the onion rings in the hot butter until golden. Lift out a few rings for garnish.

4 Add the stock and salt and pepper.

5 Put on the cover, bring steadily to H/15 lb pressure.

6 Lower the heat and cook for 3 minutes.

7 Allow pressure to drop.

8 Put the toast or bread in soup plates or soup cups.

9 Pour the soup over, garnish with onion rings and sprinkle with grated cheese.

TO VARY:

Cream of Onion Soup: Omit 280 ml (½ pt) stock. Cook to stage 6, remove cover. Blend 25 g (1 oz) flour with 140 ml (¼ pt) milk and 140 ml (¼ pt) single cream. Stir into the soup and stir until thickened. Garnish with the onion rings. The toast or bread may be added if desired.

For a more definite flavour, peel and chop or crush 2 cloves garlic. Fry these with the onion rings at stage 3. Continue as for the basic soup, but serve in flameproof soup cups or a flameproof casserole. Place under a pre-heated grill for 1–2 minutes, do not overheat the cheese.

Onion and Celery Soup: Use 340 g (12 oz) onions and 4–5 sticks celery. Fry the onions at stage 3, chop the celery and add at stage 4.

Gourmet Touch: **Soupe à L'oignon Gratinée:** Prepare the soup to stage 9, adding a little dry white wine or sherry if desired. Brown the cheese for 1–2 minutes under the grill.

PUMPKIN SOUP

Pumpkins like all squashes can be used in both sweet and savoury dishes; they make delicious soups. Since these vegetables do not have a great deal of flavour, they require generous amounts of added spices and herbs. In order to have 550 g/1¼ lb pumpkin flesh you will need to buy one weighing a good 900 g/2 lb.

Serves 4-6
Pressure cooking time 8 mins

---

1 medium onion
2 garlic cloves
1 medium carrot
550 g/1¼lb pumpkin, prepared weight
50 g /2 oz butter
½ teaspoon ground ginger, or to taste

½ teaspoon ground coriander
800 ml/1⅓ pints vegetable or chicken stock
1 teaspoon chopped sage
1 tablespoon fine chopped parsley

1   Peel and finely chop the onion, garlic and carrot. Peel the pumpkin and remove all the seeds and stringy bits and cut into chunks.

2   Heat the butter in the pan, add the onion and garlic and cook gently for 5 minutes.

3   Add the carrot, pumpkin and spices and stir over a low heat for another 5 minutes.

4   Add the stock with the herbs and a little seasoning.

5   Cover the pan, bring to H/15 lb pressure.

6   Lower the heat and cook for 8 minutes.

7   Allow pressure to drop.

8   Then sieve or liquidise the soup. Reheat before serving.

TO VARY:

Creamy Pumpkin Soup: Use the main recipe but add just ½ litre/1 pt stock. The spices can be reduced to a pinch of each. The sage can be replaced with 2 teaspoons chopped thyme. Sieve or liquidise the soup then return to the pan with 150 ml /¼ pt milk and 150 ml/¼ pt single cream. If the soup looks a little pale mix a good pinch of turmeric with the milk before adding to the puréed soup.

Pumpkin and Sesame Soup: Follow the main recipe but use 2 tablespoons sesame oil instead of the butter.

Gourmet Touch: A hotter flavour can be given to the soup if 1 deseeded, chopped red chilli is added to the other ingredients, or a good pinch of chilli powder is added to the spices.

TOMATO SOUP

Serves 4–6
Pressure cooking time 5 mins

1 medium onion
1 rasher bacon (optional)
2 sticks celery

750 g (1½ lb) tomatoes
50 g (2 oz) butter or margarine or bacon fat
Generous ½ litre (1 pt) white stock or water or ham stock
1 bay leaf
1–2 sprigs basil or parsley
Salt, pepper, paprika pepper
1 teaspoon brown sugar

TO GARNISH:
little cream, chopped chives and/or chopped basil

---

1   Peel and chop the onion, bacon, celery and tomatoes.

2   Heat the butter, margarine or fat in the open cooker, toss the bacon and vegetables in this for a few minutes; do not allow to brown.

3   Add the liquid, herbs, seasoning and sugar, fix the cover, bring to H/15 lb pressure; cook for 5 minutes.

4   Allow pressure to drop; sieve the soup, liquidising does not get rid of all the pips.

5   Top with the cream and herbs.

TO VARY:

Cream of Tomato Soup: Make the basic soup as above, but allow only 420 ml (¾ pt) stock or water. Meanwhile make a thin white sauce in a pan with 25 g (1 oz) butter or margarine, 25 g (1 oz) flour, 280 ml (½ pt) milk and 2–3 tablespoons single cream. Whisk the hot, but not boiling, tomato purée into the hot, but not boiling, sauce and serve.

Tomato and Rice Soup: Follow the basic recipe, above, allowing an extra 140 ml (¼ pt) liquid. Bring to the boil at stage 3, add 25 g (1 oz) long grain rice, and bring to the boil again, stir, and then continue as in basic recipe.

Gourmet Touch: **Iced Tomato Soup:** Make the soup as in the basic recipe, but add a small grated beetroot and 2 tablespoons sherry. Sieve and ice lightly.

SOUPS FROM PULSES

Peas, beans and lentils are an excellent source of protein, and soups made from them are not only good to eat, but also sustaining and nutritious.

LENTIL SOUP

Serves 4–6
Pressure cooking time 15 mins

---

2 or 3 sticks celery
2 medium-sized potatoes
100 g (4 oz) lentils, rinsed
Salt and pepper
Bouquet garni (see page 16) or good pinch dried mixed herbs
Generous ¾ litre (1½ pt) ham stock or water and a few bacon rinds
140 ml (¼ pt) milk or single cream

TO GARNISH:
fried croutons (see page 25)

---

1 Dice the celery, peel and dice the potatoes.

2 Put all the ingredients, except the milk or cream, into the pressure cooker.

3 Put on the cover, bring steadily to H/15 lb pressure.

4 Lower the heat and cook for 15 minutes.

5 Allow pressure to drop, remove the cover.

6 You will find lentils cooked in the pressure cooker are so tender you need not sieve the soup but just stir briskly. If you want a very smooth texture, remove the bouquet garni or herbs and bacon rinds (if used) then sieve or liquidise.

7 Return to the cooker, add the milk or cream and reheat. Serve garnished with the fried croutons.

BUTTER BEAN SOUP

Serves 6-8
Pressure cooking time 25 mins

---

225 g/8 oz dried butter beans
1.2 litres/2½ pts bacon or chicken stock
2 medium onions
2 garlic cloves
2 medium carrots
2 celery sticks

350 g/12 oz tomatoes
Pinch dried savory
1 tablespoon chopped parsley
1 teaspoon finely grated lemon rind

TO GARNISH:
soured cream

1   Wash the beans, place in the stock and soak overnight, or bring just to the boil and simmer steadily for 10 minutes. Cover the pan and allow to stand for 2–3 hours.

2   Peel and finely chop the onions and garlic; peel and slice the carrots; chop the celery and tomatoes.

3   Add to the pan of beans and stock with some seasoning, be sparing with the salt if using bacon stock. Add the herbs and lemon rind.

4   Cover the pan and bring steadily to H/15 lb pressure.

5   Lower heat and cook 25 minutes.

6   Lower pressure naturally.

7   Sieve or liquidise the soup, add a little additional stock if it is rather thick, then return to the pan and reheat. Check the seasoning and serve with soured cream

TO VARY:

Adzuki Bean Soup: These dried reddish beans make a delicious soup and have a distinctly sweet taste so you might like to add a little lemon juice to the main recipe. Follow the main recipe but use only 2 medium tomatoes and 1 garlic clove. Prepare the adzuki beans the same way as the butter beans but cook for only 15 minutes. Check the seasoning and serve.

Black Bean Soup: If possible always use bacon stock (page 26) for a soup based on these excellent black beans. Add 4 chopped streaky-bacon rashers to the other ingredients listed in the main recipe, and use 1 teaspoon ground cumin instead of savory. If you like a hot flavour, add ½ to 1 teaspoon chilli powder with the other seasoning or include 1 deseeded, chopped red chilli pepper with the rest of the ingredients, cook for 15 minutes.

Cannellini Bean Soup: Follow main recipe but use only 1 medium tomato and 1 garlic clove as cannellini beans have a very delicate flavour. Prepare the cannellini beans in the same way as butter beans but cook for only 20 minutes. This soup is delicious topped with cream cheese.

DRIED PEA SOUP

This is a really satisfying soup. You need to allow time to prepare the peas. The difference in cooking time depends upon whether using split or whole peas.

Serves 4–6
Pressure cooking time 10–20 mins

---

100 g (4 oz) split or whole dried peas
Ham stock or water (see method)
2 medium onions
1 medium carrot
1 small turnip
Salt and pepper
1 teaspoon sugar
Sprig mint or pinch dried mint

TO GARNISH:
little double cream

---

1   Soak the peas overnight in cold stock or water to cover, or put the peas into a basin, cover with boiling stock or water and leave for 1 hour.

2   Put into the pressure cooker with the liquid in which they were soaked, plus any extra needed to make up to a generous ¾ litre (1½ pt).

3   Peel and chop the onions, carrot and turnip. Add to the cooker with the other ingredients.

4   Put on the cover, bring steadily to H/15 lb pressure.

5   Lower the heat and allow 10 minutes cooking time for split peas, and 20 minutes for whole peas.

6   Allow pressure to drop.

7   Sieve or liquidise the soup and reheat if necessary. Serve each portion topped with a little cream.

TO VARY:

Haricot Bean Soup: Use 100 g (4 oz) haricot beans instead of the dried peas. Soak as instructed and use enough liquid to give 1 litre (1¾ pt) at stage 2 if using small beans; cook for 20 minutes. If using large beans, use a generous 1litre (2 pt) and cook for 30 minutes.

Gourmet Touch: Top with crisply fried diced bacon and freshly chopped mint.

Fresh Pea Soup: When peas are young and plentiful, a delicious soup can be made by cooking pods and peas together. Choose very young peas, wash and trim. Allow about 450 g (1 lb) peas and follow the ingredients in Dried Pea Soup (above); obviously no soaking is necessary. Cook for 5 minutes at H/15 lb pressure, sieve and reheat or serve cold. Top with mint leaves.

SOUPS MAKE A MEAL

The soups from pulses on the previous page, and the selection of sustaining soups that follows are ideal for a light supper or lunch.

FISH CHOWDER

Serves 4–6
Pressure cooking time 2 mins

---

2 medium onions
3 medium carrots
450 g (1 lb) white fish (hake, cod or fresh haddock)
25 g (1 oz) butter or margarine
420 ml (¾ pt) fish stock or water
Bouquet garni (see page 16) or pinch dried mixed herbs
Salt and pepper
25 g (1 oz) flour
140 ml (¼ pt) milk

TO GARNISH:
chopped parsley

---

1   Peel and grate or finely dice the onions and carrots.

2   Cut the fish into small neat pieces, removing any skin or bones.

3   Melt the butter or margarine in the cooker and fry the vegetables for 2–3 minutes, taking care they do not brown.

4   Add the stock or water, the fish, herbs and seasoning.

5   Fix the cover, bring to H/15 lb pressure.

6   Lower the heat and cook for 2 minutes.

7   Allow the pressure to drop then open the cover and remove the bouquet garni.

8 Blend the flour and milk together, add to the fish chowder and bring slowly to the boil, stirring all the time.

9 Cook gently for 2–3 minutes.

10 Garnish with chopped parsley.

TO VARY:

Bacon and Cabbage Chowder: Omit the fish, use 100–170 g (4–6 oz) bacon. Dice and fry the bacon at stage 3. Add ½ small shredded cabbage at stage 4. Use water or meat stock instead of fish stock. Top with grated cheese and chopped chives.

Gourmet Touch: **Shellfish Chowder:** Use lobster, prawns or other shellfish in place of all white fish. If these are cooked, add to the chowder at stage 8. Use half milk and half single cream at stage 8.

CHICKEN SOUPS

A really good chicken soup makes a delicious first course or even a light meal, particularly when you use some of the chicken meat. Clear chicken soups are on page 28.

One of the easiest ways to produce a chicken soup is simply to put the chicken carcass, broken into about four pieces, into the pressure cooker. Do not use the trivet, simply cover the bones with water, add a bunch of mixed herbs, or a good pinch dried herbs, salt and pepper and 1 or 2 onions and carrots, if you want a delicate vegetable flavour. You can, of course, increase the quantity and selection of vegetables to your own personal taste; and you can add 1 or 2 uncooked chicken joints to produce more chicken meat.

1 Fix the cover and bring to H/15 lb pressure.

2 Maintain this for 30–40 minutes, as though making a white stock.

3 Allow the pressure to drop then remove the cover and the bones.

You can now make one or several kinds of chicken soup.

Chicken Purée Soup: Pull all the pieces of meat from the bones. Rub these through a sieve or liquidise in the blender goblet with the stock, or stock and vegetables. You will be amazed at the thick purée produced. Taste this and add extra seasoning if required. Pour the purée back in the pan and reheat. Top with chopped parsley and serve. Allow about 200 ml (⅓ pt) per person.

Cream of Chicken Soup: Either reheat the purée, made as above, with single cream or make a white sauce while the chicken is cooking. *To make the sauce:* heat 25 g (1 oz) butter or margarine in a pan, stir in 25 g (1 oz) flour, then add 280 ml (½ pt) milk. Bring to the boil, stir until thickened. Blend this sauce into a generous 1 litre (2 pt) purée, and then add a little single cream to make the desired consistency. Allow 200–280 ml (⅓–½ pt) per person.

TURKEY SOUPS

Any of the recipes for chicken soup can be used with a turkey carcass. Since you are likely to produce more stock and purée, you could freeze the surplus to use on a future occasion. Be careful that the pressure cooker is not overfilled.

The following is an appetizing way to use turkey stock and meat left on the bones.

TURKEY AND TARRAGON SOUP

Serves 6–7
Pressure cooking time 30–40 mins

Part of a turkey carcass
Salt and pepper
2–3 medium potatoes
3–4 sticks celery
25 g (1 oz) turkey fat or butter
1–2 tablespoons chopped fresh tarragon
Pinch celery salt
Pinch garlic salt
Pinch cayenne pepper

---

1   Put the turkey carcass into the cooker with water to cover.

2   Add a *little* salt and pepper.

3   Fix the cover and bring to H/15 lb pressure.

4   Lower the heat and cook for 30–40 minutes; the longer cooking time means a richer stock.

5   Allow the pressure to drop and remove the bones and stock from the cooker.

6   Pull away any turkey flesh from the bones and chop it finely, put on one side.

7   Meanwhile peel and dice the potatoes and chop the celery.

8   Heat the turkey fat (see page 98, which describes clarifying fat) or butter in the bottom of the pressure cooker.

9   Toss the potatoes, celery and half the tarragon in the fat, do not allow the vegetables to brown.

10 Add about 1litre (1¼ pt) strained turkey stock and heat, then add the celery and garlic salt, the cayenne pepper, turkey meat and remaining tarragon. Heat and serve.

KIDNEY SOUP

Serves 4–6
Pressure cooking time see method (stage 1)

---

225 g (8 oz) kidneys (see method)
2 onions
1–2 rashers bacon
25 g (1 oz) dripping or margarine
¾ litre (1¼ pt) brown stock or water and beef stock cube
Bouquet garni (see page 16)
Salt and pepper
25 g (1 oz) flour

---

1   Finely dice the kidney: this can be lamb's kidneys, which take the shortest time to cook, i.e. 6 minutes at H/15 lb; veal or pig's kidney, which takes 7 minutes at H/15 lb; or ox kidney, which needs 15 minutes at H/15 lb pressure.

2   Peel and dice the onions; remove the rind from the bacon and dice.

3   Heat the dripping or margarine in the open pressure pan then fry the bacon, kidney and onions. Add the bacon rind to give extra flavour.

4   Add most of the stock or water and the stock cube, bouquet garni and seasoning.

5   Fix the cover, bring to H/15 lb pressure and cook for the time given in stage 1.

6   Allow the pressure to drop.

7   Blend the flour with the remaining stock or water and stir into the kidney mixture.

8   Bring to the boil and stir over a medium heat until slightly thickened. Remove the bacon rind, bouquet garni, and serve.

TO VARY:

Cream of Kidney Soup: Cook the soup to the end of stage 8. Sieve or liquidise then return to the pressure cooker with 3–4 tablespoons single or double cream. Heat gently and serve.

Devilled Kidney Soup: Blend ½–1 teaspoon curry powder with the flour at stage 7 and add ½ teaspoon made mustard and 1 teaspoon Worcestershire sauce to the liquid.

Gourmet Touch: Use a little less stock in the basic recipe or variations, add port or red wine instead.

SCOTCH BROTH

This traditional Scottish soup can make a complete light meal. While mutton is the meat usually chosen, the soup can be prepared with stewing beef. It hastens cooking time if you remove the meat from the bones (but add the bones to the liquid to add flavour). The servings depend upon whether the soup is served as a light main dish or as a first course.

Serves 4–8
Pressure cooking time 8–12 mins

---

25 g (1 oz) pearl barley
225 g (8 oz) stewing beef or 225–340 g (8–12 oz) scrag end mutton
2 medium onions
2–3 medium carrots
½ medium swede
1 medium turnip
Small piece cabbage
Generous 1 litre (2 pt) water
Salt and pepper
1–2 tablespoons chopped parsley

---

1   Blanch (whiten) the barley by putting into a basin, cover with boiling water, leave 1–2 minutes, then strain.

2   Dice the meat (remove excess fat), peel and dice the vegetables, shred the cabbage.

3   Put the meat, any bones, and vegetables into the cooker, add the water, bring to the boil, season well and then add the barley.

4   Fix the cover, bring to H/15 lb pressure.

5   Cook for 8 minutes if using diced meat, or 12 minutes if using

larger pieces on the bone.

6   Allow pressure to drop; remove the cover, take out the bones, dice meat if necessary, return to the stock.

7   Top with the parsley and serve.

TO VARY:

Leave the mutton on the bones; serve as one course and serve the vegetable broth as a separate course.

Chicken Broth: Use diced raw chicken or one or two chicken joints.

Gourmet Touch: Add 1–2 tablespoons dry sherry just before serving.

MULLIGATAWNY SOUP

Serves 4–6
Pressure cooking time 6 mins

Generous ¾ litre (1½ pt) lamb or mutton stock (see page 26)
2 medium onions
1 medium carrot
1 dessert apple
1 clove garlic (optional)
50 g (2 oz) butter or fat
1–1½ tablespoons curry powder
½–1 teaspoon dry mustard
Salt and pepper
1 tablespoon chutney
25 g (1 oz) sultanas

TO GARNISH:
chopped parsley

---

1   Strain the stock if using the recipe on page 26.

2   Peel and dice the onions, carrot and apple, then peel and crush the garlic.

3   Heat the butter or fat in the pressure cooker and toss the vegetables and apple in this for 3–4 minutes, stirring well.

4   Stir in the curry and mustard powders to taste, add the stock and the rest of the ingredients.

5   Fix the cover, bring to H/15 lb pressure and cook for 6 minutes.

6   Allow pressure to drop at room temperature.

7 To serve: top with parsley, or sieve or liquidise then reheat in the cooker and serve.

TO VARY:

The above is the classic India-type soup. If you like, add 1 tablespoon long grain rice, bring the stock to the boil at stage 4, stir in the rice then continue as in the basic recipe. Do not sieve.

To make a hotter soup add 2–3 drops chilli sauce.

Gourmet Touch: This is a delicious cold soup. Cook as above, sieve or liquidise then chill. Serve topped with yogurt or soured cream, chopped almonds and/or diced green pepper.

MINESTRONE SOUP

This is the really filling version of the Italian soup, which almost makes a meal in itself. Allow time to prepare the haricot beans.

Serves 4–6
Pressure cooking time 20–30 mins

---

75 g (3 oz) large or small haricot beans
Water or ham stock (see method)
Salt and pepper
2 medium onions
1 clove garlic (optional)
2 medium carrots
2–3 sticks celery (optional)
2 rashers streaky bacon
¼ medium cabbage
Parsley
25 g (1 oz) elbow-macaroni

TO GARNISH:
chopped parsley, Parmesan cheese

---

1 Soak the beans overnight in cold water to cover or put into a basin and cover with boiling water and leave for an hour.

2 Tip the beans with the water in which they were soaked, plus enough extra water or ham stock to give a generous ¾ litre (1½ pt), into the pressure cooker.

3 Add only a very little salt and pepper at this stage.

4 Fix the cover and bring to H/15 lb pressure.

5 Cook for about 12 minutes for small beans, but 22 minutes for large beans; allow the pressure to drop at room temperature.

6 While the beans are cooking, prepare the other ingredients; peel and chop the onions and garlic; peel and dice the carrots; chop the celery and bacon neatly, shred the cabbage.

7 Chop enough parsley to give 1–2 tablespoons plus garnish. Taste the liquid in the pan, add more salt and pepper if desired.

8 Remove the cover of the cooker, add all the other ingredients, except the garnish, fix the cover.

9 Bring once again to H/15 lb pressure, and cook for a further 8 minutes.

10 Allow pressure to drop. Serve the soup topped with chopped parsley and cheese.

Gourmet Touch: Use a little dry white wine instead of all stock.

FRUIT SOUPS

These soups are very popular in Europe, as they are deliciously refreshing in hot weather and make a pleasant change from vegetable soups.

Never make the fruit mixture too sweet, in fact, if you like an unusual, but perfectly acceptable, combination of savoury and sweet flavours, you could substitute a little stock for some of the water in the recipe that follows.

APFELSUPPE (APPLE SOUP)

This is a most refreshing soup; the flavour can be varied according to the apples chosen.

Serves 4–6
Pressure cooking time 3 mins

Scant 1 litre (1½ pt) water
1 kg (2 lb) apples
1 lemon
Salt and pepper
Sugar to taste
Good pinch ground cinnamon

---

1   Put the water into the cooker; do not use the trivet.

2   Peel and slice the apples; pare one or two large strips lemon rind from the fruit and squeeze out the juice.

3   Add the lemon rind, juice and apples to the water, with a little seasoning, sugar and cinnamon.

4   Fix the cover, bring to H/15 lb pressure.

5   Cook for 3 minutes, allow pressure to drop.

6   Remove the cover and take out the lemon rind; mash, sieve or liquidise the fruit, taste and adjust the seasoning and sugar.

7   Serve hot or cold.

TO VARY:

Cherry Plum Soup: The rather sharp, small, cherry plums make a delicious soup. Use instead of apples, and flavour with ground mace instead of cinnamon.

Other Fruits – cherries, plums, rhubarb – can be used too.

Gourmet Touch: Use half white wine or cider and half water.

CHESTNUT SOUP

Serves 4–6
Pressure cooking time 10 mins

---

450 g (1 lb) chestnuts
280 ml (½ pt) ham or white stock
Salt and cayenne pepper
280 ml (½ pt) milk
25 g (1 oz) butter or margarine

TO GARNISH:
croutons of toast or fried bread

---

1   Wash the chestnuts.

2   Put into the pressure cooker and cover with water. Do not seal the cooker.

3   Bring the water to the boil; boil steadily for 10 minutes.

4   Drain the nuts and remove the shell and brown skin while still warm.

5   Return the peeled chestnuts to the pressure cooker.

6   Add the stock, salt, and a very little pepper.

7   Put on the cover, bring steadily to H/15 lb pressure.

8   Lower the heat and cook for 10 minutes.

9   Allow pressure to drop, and then remove the cover.

10 Sieve or mash the chestnuts or liquidise with the liquid, return to the pan with the milk and butter or margarine.

11 Reheat, adding more salt and cayenne pepper to taste.

12 Garnish with the croutons.

TO VARY:

Add bacon rinds at stage 5 and remove at stage 9 or fry chopped bacon in the pan before adding the chestnuts at stage 5. Sieve or liquidise the bacon with the nuts.

Ground Nut Soup: Use 340 g (12 oz) fresh ground nuts (peanuts) in their shells, instead of chestnuts, and shell. If buying unshelled nuts, use 170–225 g (6–8 oz). Put the nuts into the pressure cooker, add 1–2 peeled, chopped onions and 1–2 tomatoes, continue as the recipe above. 25 g (1 oz) peanut butter can be used instead of butter or margarine at stage 10.

Gourmet Touch: Make the basic soup, but use single cream instead of milk. Top with tiny pieces of crisply fried bacon and chopped parsley.

COOKING FISH

Although fish is cooked comparatively quickly by ordinary methods, and indeed is often spoiled by being overcooked, there are times when it is beneficial to use the pressure cooker.

One important advantage is that you do not have the smell of fish cooking in the kitchen, or other parts of the house. The odour is kept inside the cooker. As you use comparatively little liquid when cooking fish under pressure, the fish flesh is less likely to break or lose flavour and the small quantity of liquid used in the cooker is an excellent basis for interesting sauces.

There are a number of different ways of cooking the fish. It can be steamed, poached (and adapted for a fish stew), and cooked in ways that make it similar to baked or fried fish.

POINTS TO REMEMBER

Timing: Careful timing of the pressure cooking is important just as when cooking fish by any method and guidance on this subject is given on page 52.

Choosing fish: There are many different kinds of fish, so if you cannot buy the kind suggested in the recipe then substitute a similar type. Allow approximately 170–225 g (6–8 oz) fish per person when steaming, etc. In some recipes where you have other ingredients, smaller quantities would be sufficient.

Preparation of fish: You prepare the fish just as though cooking by any other method. Add seasoning, a little lemon juice, etc., or make a stuffing. Different methods of adding interest to the fish are given in the various recipes.

Trivet: Use this when you need to lift the fish above the liquid.

Liquid: This can be water flavoured with seasoning, herbs, etc., or milk or wine according to the particular dish. Allow a minimum of at least 280 ml (½ pt) when the pressure cooking period is under 15 minutes. Increase this by another 140 ml (¼ pt) for each additional 15 minutes. Naturally, if you are poaching the fish in liquid as part of the dish the amount of liquid can be increased in accordance with the recipe.

Pressure: Unless stated to the contrary, bring up to H/15 lb pressure when cooking fish and bring to pressure quickly, unless the fish is in an ovenproof container, when it is better to bring pressure up steadily (see page 12, section 6).

Reducing pressure: Reduce the pressure under cold water, unless using an ovenproof container when you allow the pressure to drop at room temperature. This is part of the cooking time and is calculated in the recipe.

FREEZING FISH DISHES
As fish is easily spoiled by overcooking it is not likely you will want to pressure-cook and then freeze fish, but there will be many times when you may need to pressure-cook frozen raw fish. There is no need to allow this to defrost. Follow any of the recipes in this chapter, but allow one extra minute pressure cooking time for fillets or thin slices of fish. Large portions of fish or whole fish require 10–12 minutes per 450 g (1 lb), depending upon the thickness of the fish. As this may lengthen the total pressure cooking time, adjust the amount of liquid, see this page.

TIMES FOR COOKING FISH
The various ways of cooking fish, plus recipes, are given in the next pages. The average timing to allow is given below, follow this unless the recipe states to the contrary.

In addition to the times for cooking fish, ideas are given for vegetables that can be cooked in the same time, so that you end up with a complete main course. Always allow a *minimum* of 280 ml (½ pt) liquid if cooking vegetables with fish.

Fillets of plaice, sole, whiting or exceptionally thin pieces of young cod – 3 minutes at H/15 lb pressure.

Cook peas, finely diced carrots, finely diced potatoes or swedes and small flowerets or cauliflower in the separator.

Steaks of cod, fresh haddock, halibut, turbot, skate or very thin slices of salmon – 4 minutes at H/15 lb pressure.

The same vegetables as given under 'fillets' can be cooked with the fish, they can be diced slightly larger. Broccoli spears, shredded greens or whole baby turnips can also be cooked in this time.

Whole fish such as herring, trout or a fairly solid tail piece of white fish – allow 5 minutes at H/15 lb pressure.

This time enables you to cook broad or French or runner beans, halved cauliflower and small new potatoes with the fish.

Large mackerel need 6–7 minutes but when the fish above is boned, reduce the pressure cooking time by 1–2 minutes.

Whole large fish or large portions of salmon, turbot – allow 8–12 minutes, depending upon thickness of the fish, per 450 g (1 lb) at H/15 lb pressure.

It is advisable to partially cook the fish, reduce the pressure rapidly, then add the selected vegetables, bring again to pressure and continue cooking.

SAUCES TO SERVE WITH FISH

As explained throughout this book, one has to have liquid in a pressure cooker to produce the necessary steam. Often this liquid can be the basis of a first-class sauce. When the fish is cooked, remove from the cooker, keep warm, and make the sauce in the open cooker or a pan.

White Sauce: Use milk, not water in the pressure cooker.

Melt 25 g (1 oz) butter or margarine in the pan, stir in 25 g (1 oz) flour, add the liquid from the pan plus enough milk to give 280 ml (½ pt). Stir over a low heat until thickened and smooth, taste and season as necessary.

Béchamel Sauce: This is made as the white sauce, but add a piece of onion, carrot and celery to the liquid in the pressure cooker, so that the vegetables give flavour to the milk while the fish is cooking. Strain and use liquid as above. The following are based on either white or béchamel sauces:

Anchovy Sauce: Add ½ teaspoon anchovy essence to the sauce, be sparing with the salt.

Caper Sauce: Add 2–3 teaspoons capers plus 2 teaspoons vinegar or lemon juice to the hot, but not boiling, sauce.

Cheese Sauce: Add 50–100 g (2–4 oz) grated Cheddar or other cooking cheese to the thickened sauce, do not cook again.

Dill Sauce: Add 1 tablespoon chopped dill plus 2 teaspoons vinegar or lemon juice to the hot, but not boiling, sauce.

Fennel Sauce: Add 2 teaspoons chopped fennel leaves plus 2 teaspoons chopped fennel root (optional) to the sauce.

Mushroom Sauce: Simmer 50–75 g (2–3 oz) sliced mushrooms in the milk in the cooker, then make sauce.

Parsley Sauce: Add 1–2 tablespoons finely chopped parsley.

Velouté Sauce: Use all strained fish stock instead of milk.

Wine Sauce: Use half wine and half water or strained fish stock instead of milk in the cooker, then make the sauce. When thickened, remove from the heat and whisk in 3 tablespoons double cream.

Pressure Cooker Court-Bouillon: Use equal quantities of white wine and water and proceed as above. This gives a really strongly flavoured liquid.

TO 'BAKE' FISH

Although this term may not be technically correct, since baking is normally done in the oven, you can achieve much the same effect as baking if you follow the instructions below.

1   Season the fish, add any flavouring desired, then wrap in well-buttered or oiled foil or greaseproof paper.

2   Pour the correct amount of liquid, use at least 280 ml (½ pt), see page 51, into the bottom of the pressure cooker, this liquid can be flavoured or seasoned if you want to make a sauce to serve with the fish. You can read comments about the liquid to use on page 63, stage 2.

3   Place the trivet in the cooker, and the wrapped fish on top of this.

4   Fix the cover, bring rapidly to H/15 lb pressure, lower the heat and cook for the time given on page 52.

5   Reduce the pressure under cold water, unless stated to the contrary.

6   Lift out the fish and serve. If using the liquid in the cooker as part of a sauce, keep the fish warm while completing this.

TO VARY:

You may find it more convenient to cook the fish in a container, rather than wrapping it in the greaseproof paper or foil. There are several recipes using this method on this and the next page.

COD AND TOMATO SAVOURY

Serves 3–4
Pressure cooking time 4 mins

---

1 medium onion
3 medium tomatoes
2 tablespoons chopped parsley
2 tablespoons soft breadcrumbs
Salt and pepper
340 g–½ kg (12 oz–1 lb) fillet of cod

---

1 Grease a soufflé dish or small casserole.

2 Peel and grate the onion and slice the tomatoes.

3 Mix the chopped parsley, onion, tomatoes, breadcrumbs and a little salt and pepper together.

4 Put half this mixture at the bottom of the dish, and then arrange the fish on top.

5 Cover with the remainder of the tomato mixture.

6 Stand the dish on the trivet.

7 Put 280 ml (½ pt) water into the cooker.

8 Fix the cover and bring to H/15 lb pressure.

9 Lower the heat and cook for 4 minutes.

10 Allow the pressure to drop and serve with crisp toast.

TO VARY:

Use fresh haddock or hake.

Gourmet Touch: **Florentine Turbot:** Use turbot in place of cod and garnish with chopped fennel leaves. A little finely chopped white fennel could be mixed with the onion, etc. Another version of this dish is to cook spinach in the container while cooking the fish, then coat fish and spinach with cheese sauce, made as on page 53.

BASED UPON 'BAKED' FISH

The following recipes are based upon the points given in To Bake Fish, and the timings are the same as those given on page 52. Where a good weight of additional ingredients is added to the fish, the timing will be a little longer than on page 52.

Cod Jamaican: Season 4 cod steaks, brush with a little melted butter. Lay 4 small halved and seasoned bananas over the fish, wrap and cook for 4 minutes at H/15 lb pressure. Serve with:

Mustard Sauce: Use 280 ml (½ pt) milk or milk and water as the liquid in the pan. Keep the fish wrapped and keep warm, while making the sauce in the open pressure cooker. Blend 25 g (1 oz) flour, 2–3 teaspoons mustard powder with 4 tablespoons cold milk. Stir into the liquid in the cooker, add 25 g (1 oz) butter or margarine and stir over a low heat until thickened.

Other well-flavoured white fish can be used instead of cod.

Sole Jamaican: Use 4–8 fillets of sole and cook for 3 minutes at H/15 lb pressure. Serve with extra melted butter and on sauce. Garnish with watercress. Other filleted white fish can be cooked in the same way.

Fish with Anchovy Butter: Blend 50 g (2 oz) butter with 1 teaspoon anchovy essence or 4–5 chopped anchovy fillets. Season with a little black pepper and add 1–2 teaspoons chopped parsley. Spread over 4 steaks or 4–8 fillets white fish and wrap. Cook for 3–4 minutes at H/15 lb pressure.

Flavoured Butters: Instead of anchovy flavouring you can add 1 tablespoon freshly chopped herbs (fennel, dill, parsley, etc.) or 1–2 teaspoons curry powder or tomato purée, etc.

Cod en Cocotte: Put a layer of thinly sliced seasoned onions into a buttered ovenproof dish, top with 1–2 rashers chopped bacon, then 4 well-seasoned steaks of cod or other white fish. Add 3–4 tablespoons milk or fish stock or white wine. Top with more onions and bacon and a layer of thinly sliced, lightly seasoned raw potatoes. Cover with well-buttered foil. Bring pressure up steadily to H/15 lb. Cook for 12 minutes and allow to drop to room temperature.

Hake Portugaise: Peel and crush 1–2 cloves garlic; peel and chop or slice 2–3 medium onions, and skin and slice 5–6 medium tomatoes. Mix the vegetables and season well, then toss in 50 g (2 oz) melted butter or margarine. Put half the mixture into an ovenproof dish, top with 4 steaks well-seasoned hake, or other white fish, then the rest of the onion mixture. Cover with greased foil and stand on the trivet. Bring pressure up steadily to H/15 lb. Cook for 4–5 minutes and allow to drop at room temperature.

Turbot in Cream: Blend 140 ml (¼ pt) single cream with ½ teaspoon made mustard, 1–2 drops Tabasco sauce, pinch salt and pepper. Add a little chopped fennel or parsley. Put 4 portions turbot in an ovenproof dish, top with the cream mixture and cover with greased foil. Bring steadily to H/15 lb pressure, cook for 4 minutes and allow pressure to drop at room temperature.

Sole au Gratin: Fold well-seasoned fillets of sole, wrap in generously buttered foil. Bring rapidly to H/15 lb pressure, cook for 3 minutes. Reduce pressure. Put on to a flat flameproof dish, top with grated cheese, breadcrumbs and melted butter and brown for 1 minute under a hot grill.

Sole Mornay: Cook the sole as in Sole au Gratin above. Put the fish into a shallow flameproof dish. Top with cheese sauce, made as on page 53. Brown for 1 minute under a hot grill.

BROWNED FISH

This method of cooking gives fish a most attractive golden-brown appearance, usually associated with frying or grilling. The method of cooking is a combination of frying, then steaming, as on page 63. The fish, of course, will not be crisp.

1   Dry the fish well and season.

2   Heat a good knob of butter, or other fat, in the bottom of the pressure cooker, the amount depends upon the quantity of fish to be cooked: allow approximately 40 g (1½ oz) for 4 portions. Fry the fish on both sides until it becomes golden brown.

3   Remove from the cooker on to a plate or foil, spoon any fat over the fish.

4   Pour the required amount of liquid, use at least 280 ml (½ pt), see page 51, into the bottom of the cooker.

5   Add the trivet, and then place the browned fish, on the plate or foil, on the trivet.

6   Continue as for steaming, page 63, stages 4–6, but reduce the pressure cooking time by 1–2 minutes to compensate for browning the fish first.

TO VARY:

Sole Meunière: Brown whole sole or thick fillets as in stage 2, above, using 50–75 g (2–3 oz) butter. Lift on to the plate or foil. Add a little lemon juice, chopped parsley and capers to any butter remaining in the pan. Brown the butter, spoon over the sole, continue as above.

GARNISHES FOR FISH

White fish in particular can taste delicious but look rather uninteresting unless attractively garnished. Sauces, as on page 53, not only add flavour, but colour too. Make fish look inviting with garnishes of twists or slices of lemon, cucumber or tomato and sprigs of watercress or parsley. Paprika and chopped parsley or dill or fennel add flavour and colour to all fish.

BASED UPON BROWNED FISH

Liquid must be used after browning fish, see stage 4, above.

Mackerel with Gooseberry Sauce: Season whole boned mackerel. Heat 25 g (1 oz) butter in the cooker, brown the fish. Lift on to foil, place on the trivet. Put 225 g (8 oz) gooseberries with a little water and sugar into an ovenproof dish. Place in the cooker, add the liquid as in stage 4, above. Bring steadily to H/15 lb pressure, cook for 3 minutes. Allow pressure to drop at room temperature.

Skate Fines Herbes: Heat 50 g (2 oz) butter in the cooker, fry 2 small, finely chopped onions, and 50 g (2 oz) thinly sliced mushrooms in the butter, add 4 portions of skate, turn in the butter for 1–2 minutes. Lift on to foil, place on the trivet. Add 1 tablespoon chopped herbs. Cook for 2–3 minutes at H/15 lb pressure.

Trout Amandine: Season 4 fresh whole trout. Heat 50 g (2 oz) butter in the cooker and fry the trout for ½–1 minute on each side. Add 25–50 g (1–2 oz) whole blanched almonds when browning the second side. Spoon on to an ovenproof dish, stand on the trivet, bring steadily to H/15 lb pressure and cook for 2–3 minutes. Allow pressure to drop at room temperature.

Although trout is usually served this way, thick fillets of sole, steaks of cod or other white fish can be cooked in the same way.

Turbot Niçoise: Season 4 portions of turbot very lightly and flavour with a squeeze of lemon juice. Heat 50 g (2 oz) butter in the cooker and fry the turbot for a short time on each side until golden. Lift on to foil, top with thinly sliced tomatoes, ½–1 teaspoon finely chopped tarragon or parsley and tiny pieces of fresh lemon pulp. Lay 1–2 anchovy fillets on each portion of fish and cook for 2–3 minutes at H/15 lb pressure.

TO POACH FISH

1   Place the prepared fish and liquid into the pressure cooker; do not use the trivet. Check you are using sufficient liquid, you need at least 280 ml (½ pt), see page 51. Stage 2 under steaming, page 63, gives information about the choice of liquid.

2   Add seasoning and any flavouring required, some suggestions are given on this page.

3   Fix the cover, bring rapidly to H/15 lb pressure, lower the heat and cook for the time given on page 52.

4   Reduce the pressure under cold water, unless stated to the contrary.

5   Lift out the fish and serve. If using the liquid in the cooker as part of a sauce, keep the fish warm while completing this, see the recipes on pages 59 and 63.

ADVANTAGES OF POACHING FISH

This method of cooking fish in liquid is ideal for all smoked fish, and when you want the flavour of the liquid to penetrate the fish, or when cooking shellfish.

Kippers: Put these into the cooker with at least 280 ml (½ pt) water, then continue as for poaching. Allow only about 1 minute for kipper fillets (unless very thick, then allow 2 minutes, or 2–3 minutes for whole kippers). Reduce pressure, lift out fish, drain and top with butter. There is none of the very strong smell usually associated with cooking this fish. Bloaters can be cooked in the same way.

Smoked Haddock: If you like a very mild smoked haddock it is advisable to use half water and half milk as the liquid in the cooker. Put in the portions or fillets of fish or the whole smoked haddock. Follow directions for poaching allowing 3–4 minutes for thin pieces and about 7–8 minutes for a whole haddock. There is a recipe for kedgeree on page 107.

Creamed Smoked Haddock: Cook the fish as in the recipe above, and then flake. Make a white sauce, as the recipe on page 53, using some of the fish stock. Add 2–3 tablespoons double cream, the fish, and heat gently.

Other Smoked Fish: (cod, etc.) is cooked in the same way. The fish can be topped with a poached egg or just butter.

Shellfish: You will need an appreciable amount of water to cook shellfish, e.g. allow a generous 1litre (2 pt) for cooking a live lobster or crab or about ¾–1 kg (1½–2 lb) prawns. Put the shellfish into the cooker with the water, add a little salt. Follow directions for poaching and allow about 1 minute for prawns, 5–7 minutes for crab and up to 10 minutes for a large lobster. Reduce pressure and cool fish by plunging into cold water. The fish is cooked when it turns bright red. By cooling the shellfish rapidly you prevent it from becoming tough, as it could if cooled slowly.

CURRIED FISH

Serves 4
Pressure cooking time 2 mins*

---

1 small onion
1 small dessert apple
50 g (2 oz) butter or margarine or fat
½–1 tablespoon curry powder
280 ml (½ pt) water or fish stock

1 teaspoon sugar
1 tablespoon sultanas
Few drops lemon juice
Salt and pepper
4 cutlets of hake, cod or fresh haddock
25 g (1 oz) flour
140 ml (¼ pt) milk

---

1   Peel and grate the onion and apple.

2   Melt the butter or margarine or fat in the bottom of the pressure cooker.

3   Fry the onion and apple in the fat for 2–3 minutes; do not allow to brown.

4   Stir in the curry powder and cook for 1 minute.

5   Add all the other ingredients except the fish and flour and milk.

6   When the sauce comes to the boil, cook for 5 minutes without pressure.

7   Put the fish into the sauce.

8   Fix the cover, bring to H/15 lb pressure.

9   Lower the heat and cook for 2 minutes.

10 Cool the pan under cold water.

11 Blend the flour with the milk.

12 Stir into the sauce, bring slowly to the boil and simmer for 2–3 minutes, stirring all the time.

13 Serve the curried fish with cooked rice and chutney.

*   The pressure cooking time is short as the fish continues to cook in stage 12.

TO VARY:

Devilled Fish: use half the amount of curry powder, plus a little mustard powder and Worcestershire sauce.

Gourmet Touch: **Creamed Curried Fish:** Use single cream in place of milk.
Garnish with tomato, lemon and green pepper.

Fish Casserole: Omit curry powder, apple, sugar and sultanas, but increase the onions to 2 and add 2–3 grated carrots. Cook as the basic recipe, above. You can add several skinned, sliced tomatoes, in which case use all fish stock and omit milk to prevent mixture from curdling.

SOUSED FISH

Serves 4
Pressure cooking time 2–3 mins

1–2 medium onions
1–2 dessert apples (optional)
4 portions or cutlets of white fish (cod, hake, fresh haddock)
½–1 teaspoon mixed pickling spice
1–2 teaspoons sugar
½–1 teaspoon mixed spice
140 ml (¼pt) water
140 ml (¼ pt) vinegar
¼ teaspoon salt
2 bay leaves

---

1   Peel and slice the onions; core and slice but do not peel the apples, if using these.

2   Put all the ingredients into the pressure cooker, do not use the trivet.

3   Fix the cover and bring to H/15 lb pressure.

4   Lower the heat and allow 2 minutes cooking time for fairly thin portions of fish or 3 minutes for thicker pieces.

5   Cool under cold water and serve the fish hot or allow the fish to cool and serve some of the liquid as a sauce.

TO VARY:

Soused Herring or Mackerel: Split and bone the herring or mackerel, then roll from the head to the tail, secure with wooden cocktail sticks. Cook as for soused fish but allow 3–4 minutes for herring and 4–5 minutes for mackerel, depending upon the size of the fish.

Gourmet Touch: **Devilled Herring:** Peel and grate 1 small onion. Split 4 herring and take out the backbones. Cream 25 g (1 oz) butter or margarine, add ½–1 teaspoon made mustard, 2 teaspoons sugar, 2 teaspoons vinegar, 1 teaspoon Worcestershire sauce and a little salt and pepper. Spread this paste on to the herring. Roll tightly. Place the greased trivet in the cooker, add 280 ml (½ pt) water, the grated onion and ½ teaspoon mixed pickling spice. Cook as the basic recipe but allow 4 minutes. Reduce pressure; serve hot with the liquid as a sauce.

HADDOCK DUGLÈRE

Serves 4
Pressure cooking time 4 mins

---

4 large tomatoes
280 ml (½ pt) fish stock, page 26
4 portions haddock
Salt and pepper
25 g (1 oz) butter or margarine
25 g (1 oz) flour
Little milk or single cream

---

1   Skin and slice the tomatoes, put into the cooker with the strained fish stock, fish and a little seasoning.

2   Follow directions for poaching on page 58.

3   Lift out the fish and keep hot.

4   Sieve or liquidise the tomatoes with the liquid in the cooker.

5   Heat the butter or margarine, stir in the flour, and blend in the tomato purée.

6   Bring to the boil, cook until thickened, and remove from the heat, cool slightly, gradually blend in enough milk or cream to give a coating consistency. Spoon over the fish and serve with cooked potatoes or rice.

TO VARY:

Hake Maltesa: Use hake instead of haddock. Add a chopped onion, 1–2 crushed cloves garlic to the tomatoes in the pan. Omit the milk or cream at stage 6 and use a little more stock.

Cod Flamande: Use cod not haddock, omit the tomatoes and stage 4. Add 1 teaspoon made mustard, 2–3 teaspoons chopped parsley to the fish stock. Add a little grated nutmeg with the milk or cream at stage 6.

Gourmet Touch: **Sole Véronique:** Use sole instead of haddock, omit tomatoes and stage 4 from Haddock Duglère, but add 100 g (4 oz) skinned and deseeded grapes instead. You can use half stock and half white wine. Poach the fish for 2–3 minutes only at H/15 lb. Make the sauce as for Haddock Duglère, using the grapes in the liquid.

Sole Mexicaine: Follow the basic recipe using sole instead of haddock, but add 1 diced red pepper, 50 g (2 oz) sliced mushrooms, good pinch cayenne pepper to liquid and tomatoes. Omit stage 4, otherwise follow recipe for Haddock Duglère, above.

TO STEAM FISH

1 Grease the trivet, to prevent the fish from sticking. If steaming a number of fillets, which need to be piled on top of one another, separate each layer with greased greaseproof paper, so the fillets do not stick together.

2 Pour the required amount of liquid into the bottom of the cooker; use at least 280 ml (½ pt), see page 51. Choose water or fish stock for an economical sauce, or milk for a creamy sauce, or wine or dry cider for a sauce with a more subtle flavour. You can mix milk with water or fish stock, but not with wine or cider; the mixture would curdle as it heats. Add the wine or milk later to a sauce. If you do not intend using the liquid, then water should be used.

3 Put in the trivet, then place the prepared fish on this, see stage 1.

4 Fix the cover, bring rapidly to H/15 lb pressure, lower the heat and cook for the time given on page 52.

5 Reduce the pressure under cold water, unless stated to the contrary.

6 Lift out the fish and serve. If using the liquid in the cooker as part of a sauce, keep the fish warm while completing this, see the recipes on this page.

STEAMED ROES

Cod's Roe: Steam uncooked cod's roe for 4 minutes, as in method above, or until white. Slice thickly, keep warm, and then serve with a sauce (see page 53).

Cod's Roe and Bacon: Slice steamed roe thickly and fry with bacon.

Herring Roes: Steam soft or hard roes for 1 minute or slightly longer if frozen, as in method above. Serve on toast or keep hot while making a sauce (see page 53).

BASED UPON STEAMED FISH

Stuffed Fillets of Sole: Most stuffings blend with fish, although very strongly flavoured fillings tend to detract from the delicate flavour.

You can simply spread the fillets with butter and mixed herbs, or butter blended with finely grated lemon zest (yellow part of the rind), or thinly sliced seasoned tomatoes, or anchovy paste, or butter flavoured with a little anchovy essence, or curry powder, or mustard. You may prefer to make one of the suggested stuffings below. The quantities cover 4 large or 8 smaller fish fillets. When the fish is covered, roll firmly then place on buttered foil, greaseproof paper, in a buttered dish, or just on the greased trivet. Steam as in the details given on page 63, allowing 3–4 minutes at H/15 lb pressure, depending upon the thickness of the fish and filling.

Plaice or whiting fillets can be stuffed in the same way.

STUFFINGS FOR FISH

Egg and Cheese Stuffing: Hard-boil and chop 2 eggs, blend with 50 g (2 oz) grated cheese, 50 g (2 oz) melted butter, 2 tablespoons soft breadcrumbs, 1 tablespoon chopped parsley, salt and pepper.

Mushroom Stuffing: Chop 75 g (3 oz) mushrooms, blend with 25 g (1 oz) melted butter, 1–2 teaspoons chopped parsley, 2 tablespoons soft breadcrumbs, seasoning and a small egg.

Mushroom and Tomato Stuffing: As above, but replace the egg with 2 medium, skinned, chopped tomatoes.

Prawn Stuffing: Replace the mushrooms in the second recipe with 50–75 g (2–3 oz) chopped, shelled prawns.

Veal Stuffing: As on page 102.

ADVANTAGES OF STEAMING FISH

Steamed fish keeps a drier texture than poached fish, and so is ideal when fish is required for salads, moulds, fish pies and fish cakes. The steam, and the speed of cooking in the pressure cooker, prevent the fish from becoming over-dry.

FISH CAKES

Put 280 ml (½ pt) water into the cooker, you can flavour and season this to make a sauce or even use milk or fish stock. Place 225 g (8 oz) thickly sliced, peeled, old potatoes (weight when peeled), and the same weight of cod or other white fish on greased paper on the trivet and cook as steamed fish for 4–5 minutes at H/15 lb pressure. Lift out and mash the potatoes with a good knob of margarine, blend with the flaked fish. Bind with an egg or with a thick sauce made from 25 g (1 oz) butter, 25 g (1 oz) flour and 140 ml (¼ pt) liquid from the cooker. Chill slightly, then form into 8–12 round cakes, coat with seasoned flour, then beaten egg and crumbs and fry in shallow fat until crisp and brown.

FISH MOUSSE

Serves 6
Pressure cooking time see times on page 52

---

140 ml (¼ pt) white wine
140 ml (¼ pt) water
Bouquet garni (see page 16)
550 g (1¼ lb) white fish (halibut, turbot, fresh haddock, etc.)
Salt and pepper
15 g (½ oz) powdered gelatine
2 eggs
140 ml (¼ pt) double cream

TO GARNISH:
salad ingredients

---

1   Put the wine, with 140 ml (¼ pt) water and the bouquet garni into the cooker.

2   Place the fish on the greased trivet, season and steam as on page 63; the time depends upon the thickness of the fish.

3   Lift the fish from the trivet and flake finely, strain and measure the liquid, add enough water or wine to give 280 ml (½ pt) again.

4   Reheat most of this in the open cooker. Blend the gelatine with the remaining liquid and stand over a pan of boiling water, stir until dissolved.

5   Separate the egg yolks from the whites, whisk the yolks until fluffy, then add the hot gelatine liquid, gradually add the fish.

6   Allow mixture to cool and to begin to stiffen slightly.

7   Whip the cream until it just holds its shape and whisk the egg whites until very stiff.

8   Fold the cream, then the egg whites into the fish mixture, taste and adjust seasoning.

9   Spoon carefully into a 1 litre (2-pt) oiled mould and allow to set.

10 Turn out on to a bed of salad and serve with mayonnaise.

TO VARY:

Trout Mousse: Use all fresh trout, or a mixture of cooked fresh and uncooked smoked trout.

Gourmet Touch: **Salmon Mousse:** Use all cooked salmon or a mixture of white fish and flaked salmon.

SALMON À LA CONDORCET

Serves 4
Pressure cooking time 5–7 mins

---

140 ml (¼ pt) white wine
140 ml (¼ pt) water
Bouquet garni (see page 16)
50 g (2 oz) butter
¼ large cucumber
4 large tomatoes
4 steaks fresh salmon
Salt and pepper
25 g (1 oz) flour
3 tablespoons double cream

TO GARNISH:
lemon wedges

---

1   Put the wine, water and bouquet garni into the cooker.

2   Spread a piece of foil with half the butter, melt the remainder.

3   Peel the cucumber and tomatoes, and slice thickly.

4   Put the trivet, then the foil into the cooker, top with the salmon, cucumber and tomatoes.

5   Season lightly, spoon the melted butter over the top then continue as for steaming, page 63, allowing 5–7 minutes at H/15 lb pressure, depending upon the thickness of the fish.

6   Lift the vegetables on to a hot dish, top with the salmon.

7   Strain the liquid and make the sauce as for wine sauce, page 53, adding the cream when thickened.

8   Spoon the sauce over the fish, garnish with lemon.

COOKING MEAT, POULTRY AND GAME

A pressure cooker is ideal for cooking meats, poultry and game. It saves you a great deal of cooking time and produces appetizing dishes, often from cheaper cuts of meat or older fowl which can be so difficult to tenderize but which, when cooked under pressure, become succulent and moist.

The liquid in the cooker will vary with the dish, but even water, or water flavoured with a stock cube, acquires a delicious flavour as it absorbs the meat juices during cooking, thus enabling you to make gravies and sauces that enhance the dish.

POINTS TO REMEMBER

Timing: When boiling or pot roasting, you time the cooking period by weight just as you do by any other method, i.e. so much time per 450 g (1 lb). The only difference is that the total cooking time in a pressure cooker is appreciably shorter than when boiling in a saucepan or roasting in the oven. When making a stew or braising, total cooking time, again, is much shorter than when cooking by saucepan method.

Choosing meats, etc.: In order to get the best result from a particular recipe, a suggested cut or type of meat or poultry is given. If you change this then you may have to alter the cooking times slightly. If you buy a more tender piece of meat or a younger chicken, shorten the cooking time. If, on the other hand, you select a less choice piece of meat or an older fowl, then allow slightly longer in the pressure cooker. Quantities to allow are in the recipes or introductions to methods of cooking.

Preparation of meat, etc.: The recipe will suggest the way in which the food is prepared, i.e. sliced, diced, jointed, etc. It is wise to follow these recommendations as they may affect the appearance and/or cooking time of the dish.

Trivet: Use this when you need to lift the meat, poultry or game above the level of the liquid.

Pressure: Unless stated to the contrary, bring up to H/15 lb pressure when cooking meat and bring to pressure quickly, unless the meat is in an ovenproof container, when it is better to bring pressure up steadily (see page 12).

Reducing pressure: Reduce the pressure under cold water, unless using an ovenproof container, when you allow the pressure to drop at room temperature. This is part of the cooking time and is calculated in the recipe.

ADDING INGREDIENTS TO THE MEAT

In some recipes the onions and/or other vegetables are put into the cooker at the same time as the meat. This means they give flavouring to the meat, and to the liquid which forms the sauce or gravy. In other recipes the vegetables are added *during* cooking. Just reduce pressure, add the vegetables, bring once again to pressure and continue cooking for a short period. The vegetables retain their texture and can be served as a garnish. On many occasions you will cook vegetables to serve *with* the stew, pot roast, etc. In this case, check the cooking time on pages 111-115, reduce the pressure at the right time, and place the container of vegetables into the cooker; complete the cooking time for the meat so the whole main course is ready at the same time. If serving rice or pasta, see comments on pages 120-122. The reducing of pressure and addition of the extra ingredients is little more trouble than taking the lid off a saucepan.

FREEZING MEAT, POULTRY AND GAME

There are two ways in which the pressure cooker can be used in conjunction with the freezer in preparing meat, poultry and game.

a) You can cook some of these foods by pressure without defrosting, as outlined below.

b) You can pressure-cook stews and similar dishes, cool, pack and freeze, then use the pressure cooker to reheat the food when required.

DEALING WITH FROZEN RAW MEAT

Diced meat for stews, etc.: There is no need to defrost before cooking. If the recipe requires the meat to be tossed in fat before adding liquid, etc., do this in the open cooker over a low heat to prevent splashing, stir, and the meat will separate, then proceed as the recipe. If the recipe adds liquid, without frying first, put the block of frozen meat into the cooker, add the liquid, approximately 420 ml (¾ pt), seasoning and other ingredients. Bring cooker to H/15 lb pressure, cook for 5 minutes longer than when using fresh meat.

Minced meat: Allow this to defrost sufficiently to separate into smaller pieces if using method of cooking on page 73, or brown as above (under diced meat) then proceed as the recipe.

Joints: a) Pot roasting; although you can cook from the frozen state, I find it better to allow lamb and bacon to thaw out before cooking (although they can be pot roasted from frozen). Beef I find better cooked from the frozen stage, rather than allowing it to thaw. Naturally the timing will be longer if the joint is frozen. Brown the meat and proceed as on page 97, but allow an extra 8–9 minutes per 450 g (1 lb). Adjust the amount of liquid for the longer cooking time.

(b) When boiling joints of meat, cook from the frozen state allowing an extra 10 minutes per 450 g (1 lb).

Poultry and Game: Whole birds must be *completely* defrosted before cooking. Allow at least 24 hours in the refrigerator for a medium-sized bird to thaw out. Joints of raw poultry can be cooked from the frozen stage, see diced meat.

Meat puddings and moulds: Allow to thaw out for at least 12 hours and cook or reheat as in recipes on pages 94 and 98.

PREPARING DISHES FOR FREEZING

Take particular care that the stew is not overcooked if you intend to freeze it. I generally deduct 2–3 minutes from the total pressure cooking time, for the food re-cooks slightly as it is reheated.

If you are cooking the dish to eat some on the same day and freeze the rest, then follow instructions above, remove the amount required to freeze, bring the cooker once again to pressure and completely cook the remainder of the food. It is better to thicken sauces, etc., when reheating, rather than before freezing.

TO REHEAT FROZEN STEWS

Put 280 ml (½ pt) water or other liquid into the cooker, unwrap the food, place in the cooker in the frozen stage. Bring to H/15 lb pressure, and cook for 5–12 minutes, depending upon the quantity of food. The sauce may be thinner than usual, so you might wish to simmer the mixture for a few minutes in the open pan, to evaporate some before thickening.

The other way to deal with frozen stews is to allow them to defrost then spoon the food into the cooker, bring to H/15 lb pressure, cook for 1–2 minutes only and reduce pressure immediately. Note: Cool the cooker under cold water to avoid overcooking meat.

MAKING A STEW

Some of the most interesting dishes from meat, poultry or game are stews of various kinds. These give you a great opportunity to use your own imagination and to combine a variety of vegetables, herbs, etc., with the meats. You save an almost unbelievable amount of time in cooking, for the food is ready in minutes, rather than hours, as you will see from the recipes which follow. A stew uses meat economically, allow from 100 g (4 oz) per person.

FOR A PERFECT STEW

Frying meat, etc.: Most meats are better if they are first browned in a little hot dripping, fat or butter, etc. Do not use a frying pan for this purpose but the base of the pressure cooker. In this way none of the fat is wasted, as it combines with the liquid to give a good stock.

Coating meat, etc.: In a pressure cooker you do not coat the meat or poultry or game with flour before frying, but thicken the gravy at the end of the cooking time. This is easily done, as you will see from the recipes. Simply blend the flour, or cornflour, with cold liquid. Stir this into the gravy and continue stirring over a steady heat until the sauce is smooth and of the right consistency. If the recipe states 25 g (1 oz) flour and you want to use cornflour, simply substitute half the amount, i.e. nearly 15 g (½ oz) cornflour.

Trivet: This is not used in stewing, as the food is cooked in the liquid.

Liquid: Choose water or stock or add a little wine if desired. When you consider the amount of liquid that evaporates during the normal long process of stewing in a saucepan, or cooking in a casserole in the oven, you will realize that is why only about two-thirds the usual amount of liquid is used.

Pressure: Bring rapidly to H/15 lb. Lower the heat, cook as recipe.

Reducing pressure: Under cold water.

STEWED STEAK

Serves 4–5
Pressure cooking time 15 mins

450-750 g (1–1½ lb) stewing steak (choose inexpensive cuts of meat)
Salt and pepper
2 medium onions

4 medium carrots
1–2 medium turnips
40 g (1 oz) dripping or fat
420 ml (¾ pt) stock or water with 1 stock cube
Bouquet garni (see page 16)
25 g (1 oz) flour

---

1 Cut the meat into neat cubes, or fingers, approximately 2 cm (1 in) in size, season lightly.

2 Peel and slice or dice the vegetables neatly.

3 Heat the fat in the cooker and toss first the onions and then the meat in the fat.

4 Add all the liquid except 3–4 tablespoons, stir well to absorb the juices from the bottom of the cooker.

5 Put in the rest of the vegetables, and the bouquet garni (herbs tied in a piece of muslin or in a bunch with cotton or string).

6 Fix the cover, bring rapidly to H/15 lb pressure.

7 Lower the heat and cook for approximately 15 minutes, the time depends on the size of the pieces and quality of the meat, but test after this time.

8 Reduce the pressure, then blend the flour with the remaining liquid, stir into the hot stock and continue stirring over a medium heat until thickened. Taste and add more seasoning if desired.

9 Remove the bouquet garni and serve.

BASED ON STEWED STEAK

Steak and Kidney: Omit the carrots and turnips, use 100–170 g (4–6 oz) diced ox kidney instead. The onions also can be omitted. The meat should be cooked and the gravy thickened as in the recipe for stewed steak.

Steak and Kidney Pie: Cook the steak and kidney as above, but shorten the time at H/15 lb pressure by 1 minute, so the meat is slightly firm. Lift the meat from the cooker with a perforated spoon, so you do not use too much thickened gravy. Put into a generous 1 litre (2-pt) pie dish. Cool slightly, then top with short crust or flaky pastry made with 170 g (6 oz) flour, etc. Bake for approximately 35–40 minutes in the centre of a hot to very hot oven (depending upon type of pastry used), 220–230°C (425–450°F), Gas Mark 7–8, reduce the heat after 20 minutes. Heat the rest of the gravy and serve with the pie. Mushrooms can be added to the meat before thickening the gravy.

Flemish Stew: Follow recipe for the stewed steak, page 70-71, use 4–5 skinned sliced tomatoes, omit the carrots and turnips. Omit the flour, thicken the stew with 1 slice bread, spread with made mustard. Drop into the hot stock, simmer for 2 minutes; beat hard until bread is absorbed by the liquid.

Gourmet Touch: These simple stews are excellent if you use a little beer in place of some stock or water and a stock cube.

Veal Marengo: Use stewing veal in place of beef, and half white wine and half white stock, see recipe on page 70-71. Add 50 g (2 oz) small button mushrooms plus 1 tablespoon tomato purée to the liquid before thickening at stage 8.

Wellington Casserole: Use stewing lamb instead of beef. Prepare and cook as stewed steak on pages 70-71, adding sliced celery to the other vegetables, and ½ teaspoon rosemary. Garnish with chopped parsley.

Flavourings for Stews: A pinch of curry powder, or a teaspoon Worcestershire or soy sauce, or yeast extract can be added for extra flavour.

BEEF AND VEGETABLE STEW

Serves 8
Pressure cooking time 15 mins

---

3 tablespoons oil
1 kg/2 lb stewing beef
200 g/7 oz onions, chopped
200 g/7 oz each of leeks, carrots, green beans, celery, finely chopped
200 g/7 oz fresh peas
500 g/1 lb potatoes, diced
1 litre/2 pts beef stock

---

1 Dice the beef and fry in the oil until browned.
2 Add chopped onions, vegetables and potatoes.
3 Season and add hot stock.
4 Place on cover and bring to H/15 lb.
5 Cook for 15 minutes.

SAVOURY MINCE

Serves 4
Pressure cooking time 5–6 mins

---

2 medium onions
3 medium tomatoes
Approximately 225 g (8 oz) root vegetables (optional)
25–50 g (1–2 oz) fat
Generous 280 ml (½ pt) brown stock
450 g (1 lb) minced raw beef
Salt and pepper
25 g (1 oz) flour
2–4 slices toast

---

1   Peel and slice the onions and tomatoes, peel and dice the root vegetables.

2   Heat the fat in the open pan, fry the onions and tomatoes for 2–3 minutes; some people like the meat fried at this stage, but I prefer to add it after the liquid.

3   Pour in 280 ml (½ pt) stock, add the meat, stir as the liquid comes to the boil, to give a smooth texture, season, cook for 5–6 minutes, depending upon the quality of the meat, reduce the pressure.

4   Blend the flour with the remaining liquid, stir into the mince and cook steadily until thickened.

5   Serve with toast or cooked rice (see page 120), or potatoes.

TO VARY:

Curried Mince: Add 1–2 teaspoons curry powder plus 1 teaspoon sugar to the onions and tomatoes, and 25 g (1 oz) sultanas to the stock.

Creamed Mince: Omit the tomatoes, and flavour with a little grated lemon rind and mixed herbs. Blend the flour with 4–5 tablespoons single cream and thicken as above.

Gourmet Touch: **Chilli Con Carne:** Fry a chopped green pepper and 2–3 sticks chopped celery with the onions and tomatoes. Stir in *from* ½ teaspoon chilli powder, proceed as in the basic recipe but omit the root vegetables. Taste the mixture before fixing the cover, add more chilli powder if desired. When cooked, heat 225 g (8 oz) haricot beans, cooked as on page 116-117, with the mince. Or you could use a drained tin of red kidney beans. See also the recipe for Bolognese Sauce, page 104.

IRISH STEW

Serves 4
Pressure cooking time 12 mins

---

1 kg (2 lb) scrag end or middle neck of mutton*
450-750 g (1–1½ lb) potatoes
4–6 medium onions
280 ml (½ pt) water
Salt and pepper

TO GARNISH:
chopped parsley
*You may need a little more meat as the bones weigh heavily.

---

1   Cut the mutton into neat pieces, if the butcher has not already done this.

2   Peel the potatoes; if small, leave whole, if large, cut into thick slices. Peel and slice the onions fairly thickly too.

3   Arrange the meat then the potatoes and sliced onions in the pressure pan.

4   Add the liquid and salt and pepper to taste.

5   Fix the cover, bring to H/15 lb pressure.

6   Lower the heat and cook for 12 minutes.

7   Cool under cold water.

8   Arrange the meat and vegetables on a hot dish, top with chopped parsley. Serve with the unthickened liquid as a sauce.

TO VARY:

Lancashire Hotpot: While you could cook the layers of meat, etc., in a dish in the cooker it is quicker to cook as above then lift into a flameproof dish, ending with a layer of potatoes. Moisten with a little stock, brush with melted butter and brown under the grill.

Gourmet Touch: **Saffron Lamb:** Use best end of neck of lamb in the Irish Stew, and half stock and half white wine. Allow 10 minutes at H/15 lb pressure. Lift the well-drained meat and vegetables on to a hot dish. Blend 140 ml (¼ pt) stock with 140 ml (¼ pt) double cream and ½ teaspoon saffron powder. Heat gently then spoon over the meat, etc.

BASED ON IRISH STEW

The recipes on this page are those where the liquid is not thickened or where potatoes tend to form a natural thickening.

Goulash: While this can be made with one kind of meat, i.e. beef or veal, it is more interesting if you use about 170 g (6 oz) stewing beef, 170 g (6 oz) stewing veal and 170 g (6 oz) lean pork. Dice the meats, then peel and slice 3–4 onions. Toss the meats with the onions in 50 g (2 oz) hot fat in the open cooker. Add a large can of plum tomatoes (these give the best flavour) with liquid, salt, pepper and 1–2 tablespoons paprika (this is the sweet, not hot, pepper), together with 280 ml (½ pt) white stock. Fix the cover, bring to H/15 lb pressure. Cook for 15 minutes if using the mixture of meats of all veal or all pork, but only 10 minutes with good quality stewing steak alone. Reduce the pressure, then add 450 g (1 lb) peeled sliced potatoes, stir into the tomato mixture; check there is sufficient liquid. Bring once again to H/15 lb pressure and cook for 4 minutes. Reduce pressure and serve topped with yogurt and chopped parsley. If you wish to use a little extra stock you may have some of the sauce left and this makes an interesting soup.

Tajine Tfaia: This Moroccan dish makes a delicious change. Use lamb cut from the leg or shoulder, or you could use the cheaper cuts as in Irish Stew, above. Allow a generous 500 g (1¼ lb) lamb (weight without bones). Dice the meat and roll in a mixture of ¼ teaspoon ground ginger, ¼ teaspoon powdered saffron, the grated rind of 1 lemon, salt and pepper. Peel and slice 2–3 onions. Heat 50 g (2 oz) butter in the open pan. Fry the meat with the onions for a few minutes, add 280 ml (½ pt) white stock. Cook at H/15 lb pressure for 10 minutes for tender lamb, or 12 minutes as in Irish Stew for cheaper cuts. Serve with cooked rice (see page 120).

SWEET AND SOUR SPARE RIBS

Serves 6-8
Pressure cooking time 12 mins

1.5 kg/3 lb pork spare ribs, cut into separate ribs
2 teaspoons dry mustard
1 teaspoon salt
1 tablespoon oil
2 tablespoons brown sugar
250 ml/9 fl oz sherry

1 tablespoon soy sauce
1 tablespoon rice vinegar
1 tablespoon ground ginger

1   Rub the ribs with the mustard and season with salt.

2   Heat oil in the cooker and brown the ribs, in batches.

3   Return all the meat to the pan, sprinkle in sugar and stir.

4   Combine sherry, soy sauce, vinegar and ginger.

5   Pour over meat and stir to coat the ribs.

6   Close cooker and bring to H/15 lb.

7   Cook for 12 minutes.

BEEF OLIVES

Serves 4
Pressure cooking time 15–18 mins

Veal stuffing (see page 102)
450 g (1 lb) stewing steak or topside of beef, cut in 4 large thin slices
40–50 g (1½–2 oz) fat or dripping
420 ml (¾ pt) stock or water and 1 stock cube
Bay leaf
Salt and pepper
25 g (1 oz) flour

TO GARNISH:
macédoine of vegetables (carrots, turnips, onions, beans, peas, etc., see stage 10)

1   Make the stuffing as on page 102.

2   Flatten the meat with a rolling pin; if the slices are very large, halve each slice.

3   Spread the stuffing in the centre of each piece of meat.

4   Roll firmly and secure with wooden cocktail sticks, strong cotton or fine string.

5   Heat the fat or dripping in the bottom of the pressure cooker.

6   Fry the rolls of meat until golden brown. (Turn carefully so they do not break.)

7 Add most of the liquid, the bay leaf and salt and pepper.

8 Fix the cover and bring to H/15 lb pressure.

9 Lower the heat, cook for 12–15 minutes depending upon the tenderness of the meat, and reduce pressure.

10 Prepare the vegetables while the meat is cooking, i.e. peel, and dice, or shell peas, etc., put into container.

11 Bring again to H/15 lb and cook for a further 3 minutes.

12 Reduce the pressure, lift the beef olives on to a hot dish, remove the sticks, cotton or string, then spoon the vegetables round the meat.

13 Blend the flour with the remaining liquid, stir into the stock and stir over a low heat until thickened, remove the bay leaf.

14 Pour some sauce over the beef olives, serve the rest separately.

TO VARY: Use wine or beer in the liquid.

VEAL BIRDS:

Follow the recipe for Beef Olives but use thin slices of veal instead of beef, butter in place of fat, and white, not brown, stock.

Gourmet Touch: Serve Veal Birds with a creamy sauce. Use only 280 ml (½ pt) white stock and 2 tablespoons dry sherry in cooking the meat. Blend the flour with 140 ml (¼ pt) single cream at stage 13, cook over a low heat, stirring continually, until the sauce thickens.

BLANQUETTE OF VEAL

Serves 4
Pressure cooking time 12 mins

Generous 500 g (1¼ lb) stewing veal
2 onions
50 g (2 oz) butter
Generous 280 ml (½ pt) white stock
Bouquet garni (see page 16)
Salt and pepper
25 g (1 oz) flour
140 ml (¼ pt) milk or single cream
1 or 2 egg yolks
1 tablespoon lemon juice

---

1   Cut the meat into neat fingers, peel and slice the onions.

2   Heat the butter in the open cooker, fry the meat and onions for 1–2 minutes, do not brown.

3   Add the stock, bouquet garni, seasoning, cook for 12 minutes at H/15 lb pressure, reduce pressure.

4   Remove the bouquet garni, blend the flour with half the milk or cream, add to the stock, stir over a low heat until thickened.

5   Blend the rest of the milk or cream, egg yolk(s) and lemon juice, whisk into the hot sauce, heat gently for 2–3 minutes.

6   Serve with cooked rice (page 120).

TO VARY:

Blanquette of Rabbit: Use a young rabbit instead of veal. Allow 20 minutes at H/15 lb pressure (stage 3).

Blanquette of Chicken or Guinea Fowl: Joint a young chicken or fowl, cook as above. Allow 5–6 minutes at H/15 lb pressure (stage 3).

RAGOÛT OF VENISON

This venison ragoût could be a standard recipe for all other game. There is no need to marinate venison before using the meat in a ragoût, but I find the flavour is better if the game is cooked one day, left overnight in the refrigerator then warmed through thoroughly before serving on the following day.

Serves 4–6
Pressure cooking time 15 mins

---

750 g–1 kg (1½–2 lb) venison
About 24 small onions or shallots or 2–3 large onions
300 g (12 oz) small young carrots or 4–5 large carrots
50 g (2 oz) beef dripping or fat
420 ml (¾ pt) brown stock or water and 1½ beef stock cubes
Salt and pepper
Pinch dried or ½–1 teaspoon chopped fresh sage
25 g (1 oz) flour
6 tablespoons red wine

---

1   Cut the venison into neat pieces.

2   Peel the onions or shallots and carrots, slice large onions and carrots rather thickly.

3   Heat the dripping or fat in the open cooker and fry the venison and onions together for a few minutes until the latter are golden brown. Then remove the onions from the pressure cooker.

4   Add the stock or water and stock cubes, seasoning and sage.

5   Fix the cover and bring to H/15 lb pressure, cook for 10 minutes then reduce the pressure and add the onions and carrots.

6   Bring once again to H/15 lb pressure, cook for 5 minutes then reduce the pressure.

7   Blend the flour and wine, stir into the stock in the cooker and cook over a low heat until thickened.

8   Serve with redcurrant jelly.

TO VARY:

Add 2–3 tablespoons redcurrant jelly to the sauce.

Use 280 ml (½ pt) stock, 140 ml (¼ pt) juice from canned red cherries; add cherries to the sauce before serving.

Add 12 stuffed or black or green olives to the sauce before serving.

BASED ON RAGOÛT OF VENISON

Jugged Hare: Use a jointed hare in place of the venison in the recipe with the same amount of vegetables and liquid. Ask for the blood and liver of the hare. Wash the hare in cold water, dry, and then fry with the prepared onions in the open cooker. Blend the blood and stock, pour over the hare and onions. Add the sliced carrots, hare liver, seasoning and sage. Fix the cover, bring to H/15 lb pressure and cook for 25–30 minutes for a young hare or 35–40 minutes for an older one. Reduce the pressure, lift the pieces of hare from the liquid.

Sieve or liquidise liquid, return to the open cooker. Blend 25 g (1 oz) flour with 4–5 tablespoons port wine or stock, add to the sauce, together with 2–3 tablespoons redcurrant jelly. Stir over a low heat until thickened and smooth. Return the hare to the sauce, heat in the open cooker.

Serve garnished with fried bread and with redcurrant jelly.

TO VARY:

Cook small dumplings (see recipe on page 100) in the thickened sauce. Check there is enough liquid.

Jugged Rabbit: Use the same recipe as above but allow only 20 minutes at H/15 lb.

Ragoût of Oxtail: Use 1 large or 2 smaller oxtails in place of the venison in the recipe. Ask the butcher to joint the tail(s) neatly. Fry the oxtail with the onions as in stage 3. As oxtail contains a considerable amount of natural fat, remove any excess fat after removing the onions from the cooker (stage 3). Continue as in the recipe but cook for 30 minutes at stage 5. Add the vegetables, bring once more to H/15 lb pressure and continue cooking for a further 5 minutes.

TO VARY:

Add 3–4 skinned, sliced tomatoes at stage 6 and 50 g (2 oz) haricot beans, cooked as on page 116-117.

CHICKEN CHASSEUR

Serves 4–6
Pressure cooking time 5 mins

---

1 young roasting chicken
Salt and pepper
100 g (4 oz) mushrooms
1 large onion
3–4 tomatoes
50 g (2 oz) butter
1 tablespoon oil
140 ml (¼ pt) white wine
140 ml (¼ pt) white stock
½ tablespoon chopped tarragon
½ teaspoon chopped parsley or chervil
25 g (1 oz) flour

---

1   Cut the chicken into neat joints, season well.

2   Wash and slice the mushrooms, do not peel; peel and chop or slice the onion; skin and chop the tomatoes or these can be sieved to make a purée before cooking.

3   Heat the butter and oil in the open cooker, fry the chicken until golden brown, and remove from the cooker.

4   Fry the onion and mushrooms for 1 minute only, replace the chicken and add the wine, tomatoes or tomato purée, most of the stock and the herbs.

5   Fix the cover, bring to H/15 lb pressure and cook for 5 minutes.

6   Reduce pressure, and then blend the flour and remaining stock.

7   Stir into the sauce and continue stirring over a low heat until thickened and smooth. Add more seasoning if desired. If cooking for one person, it is not essential to thicken the sauce.

TO VARY:

Use ready-jointed young chicken in this and the recipe below. If frozen, there is no need to defrost.

Pollo alla Cacciatore: The Italian version of this dish is given a more piquant flavour by adding 1 teaspoon chopped fresh oregano or marjoram at stage 4, together with a pinch of powdered cloves.

The Chasseur mixture, made in stages 2, 4, 5, 6, and 7 is an excellent sauce in which to heat left-over cooked chicken or turkey.

COQ AU VIN

Obviously your choice of wine determines the appearance and flavour of the dish – try it with both red or white wine in turn.

Serves 4–6
Pressure cooking time 5 mins

---

1 young roasting chicken (a cock bird if possible)
100 g (4 oz) button mushrooms
8 small onions or shallots
1–2 cloves garlic
100 g (4 oz) bacon or pancetta (in one piece)
50 g (2 oz) butter
280 ml (½ pt) red or white wine
Salt and pepper
25 g (1 oz) flour
2–3 tablespoons stock

---

1   Cut the chicken into neat joints, do not season at this stage.
2   Trim the stalks of the mushrooms – wash but do not peel. Peel the onions or shallots but leave them whole; peel and crush the garlic; dice the bacon or pork.
3   Heat the butter in the open cooker and fry the bacon and vegetables until the onions are golden; spoon out of the cooker.
4   Add the chicken and cook over a low heat until golden brown.
5   Replace the bacon and vegetables, add the wine and seasoning.
6   Fix the cover, bring to H/15 lb pressure and cook for 5 minutes.

Reduce pressure.

7   Blend the flour and stock, stir into the liquid in the pan and continue stirring over a low heat until thickened and smooth. Taste the sauce and add more seasoning if required.

TO VARY:

Gourmet Touch: **Poulet à la Marengo:** Follow the directions above but add a crushed garlic clove to the onions at stage 3 and blend ½–1 tablespoon tomato purée into the wine at stage 5. Stir a few olives and the flesh from a small cooked or canned lobster into the thickened sauce at stage 7. Heat for 1–2 minutes. Put on to a hot dish and top with croutons of fried bread and 4–6 fried eggs.

CREAMED TRIPE AND ONIONS

Serves 4–6
Pressure cooking time 10–15 mins

---

1 kg (2 lb) tripe
3–4 onions
25 g (1 oz) butter
140 ml (¼ pt) white stock
140 ml (¼ pt) milk
Salt and pepper
25 g (1 oz) flour
4–5 tablespoons milk or single cream

TO GARNISH:
paprika, chopped parsley

---

1   Cut the tripe into fingers.

2   Put into the open cooker with water to cover, bring to boiling point, then strain the tripe, and discard the water.

3   Peel and slice the onions.

4   Heat the butter in the open pressure cooker, toss the onions in this for 1–2 minutes.

5   Add the stock, milk, tripe and seasoning.

6   Fix the cover, bring to H/15 lb pressure, and cook for 10 minutes if the tripe is thick.

7   Reduce the pressure, blend the flour with the extra milk or

cream, stir into the liquid and stir over a low heat until thickened.

8   Serve topped with paprika and parsley.

TO VARY:

Always prepare tripe as in stages 1 and 2 and follow the cooking times as given in stage 6.

Ragoût of Tripe: Follow recipe for Ragoût of Venison, page 78.

Tripe Rolls: Follow the recipe for Beef Olives on page 76 – this is a delicious dish.

Tripe Niçoise: Use all tomato juice in the basic recipe instead of stock and milk.

Gourmet Touch: **Tripe au Gratin:** Stir 50–100 g (2–4 oz) grated cheese into the sauce after thickening, stage 7. Spoon into a flame-proof dish. Top with grated cheese, breadcrumbs and a little butter, brown under a hot grill.

BRAISING

Braising is not another term for stewing, although quite often one is served with 'braised' meats or 'braised' vegetables which have been stewed in liquid. When foods are braised they are first browned in hot fat, and then lifted out of the pan.

You then put in a layer of diced vegetables, etc., which is known as a 'mirepoix', plus a small amount of liquid. You will need a minimum of 280 ml (½ pt) or enough to come halfway up the layer of vegetables (whichever is the greater amount). The meat, game or poultry or large vegetables, such as onions or celery hearts, are then placed above the mirepoix, so that while they absorb flavour and moisture from this, they are never immersed in liquid. A pressure cooker is ideal for braising and you will be delighted with the flavour; especially the rich flavour and tender texture produced in the less expensive cuts of meat.

Recipes for braised foods are on pages 84 and 88.

Trivet: Normally one does not use a trivet, for the mirepoix lifts the meat, etc., above the liquid. If you are rather short of vegetables you could put the trivet over these to hold the meat, or other food, above the level of the liquid.

Liquid: See the comments above. The liquid can be water, wine or cider.

Pressure: Bring rapidly to H/15 lb pressure when braising, lower the heat and cook for stated time.

Reducing pressure: Reduce the pressure under cold water.

BRAISED VEGETABLES

Whole large onions, celery hearts and leeks can be braised in a similar way to the meats that follow. The cooking time can be found on pages 113-114, but first brown the vegetables in hot fat in the open cooker, and then prepare a mirepoix as suggested below.

BRAISED HEART

Serves 4–6
Pressure cooking time 15–20 mins*

450-750 g (1–1½ lb) ox heart or sheep hearts
Salt and pepper

FOR THE MIREPOIX:
2–3 onions
2–3 carrots
1 small turnip
50 g (2 oz) fat or dripping
Bouquet garni (see page 16) or ¼ teaspoon mixed dried herbs
Good 280 ml (1/2 pt) brown stock or water and 1/2 stock cube
(see page 25)

---

1   Cut the heart into thick (about 1-cm/½-in) slices, season lightly. Peel and dice or slice the vegetables.

2   Heat the fat or dripping in the bottom of the pressure cooker.

3   Fry the sliced heart in the hot fat until brown, do not overcook; lift out of the pan, pour away all fat except 1 tablespoon.

4   Add all the other ingredients, season lightly, and then place the heart on top of the vegetables and liquid.

5   Fix the cover and bring to H/15 lb pressure.

6   Cook for 15 minutes, and then reduce the pressure under cold water.

7   Lift the heart from the cooker, put on to a hot dish, and remove the bouquet garni.

8   Sieve or liquidise the vegetable mixture and serve as a sauce over the

meat, or serve the vegetables and liquid as a garnish round the meat.

*Note: Some ox heart needs 20 minutes cooking.

TO VARY:

The small amount of liquid from the mirepoix could be thickened with 1–2 teaspoons flour if desired; do this after removing meat and vegetables from the pan, see stage 8 above. Fry 1–2 diced rashers of streaky bacon with the sliced heart.

Gourmet Touch: **Mock Braised Duckling:** Add juice and grated rind of 1 orange and 2 tablespoons red wine to the mirepoix. Serve with sage and onion stuffing, page 101, (cooked in covered container).

BRAISED LIVER

Serves 4
Pressure cooking time 15 mins

---

340 g (¾ lb) ox liver
Salt and pepper

FOR THE MIREPOIX:
3 onions
2 tomatoes
2 rashers streaky bacon
25 g (1 oz) dripping or fat
280 ml (½ pt) beef stock or water and ½ stock cube
½ teaspoon chopped sage or pinch dried sage

TO GARNISH:
chopped parsley

---

1   Cut the liver into thick (1-cm/½-in) slices, season lightly.

2   Cut the onions and tomatoes into thick slices, dice the bacon.

3   Heat the dripping or fat in the bottom of the pressure cooker, add the diced bacon.

4   Fry the liver and onions until just brown, lift out of the pan, remove all fat except 1 tablespoon.

5   Add all the mirepoix ingredients, including the stock and sage, to the bacon in the bottom of the pan, season lightly, place the liver on top.

6   Fix the cover, bring to H/15 lb pressure, then follow stages 6–8 in Braised Heart. Garnish with the parsley.

TO VARY:

Braised Ox Kidney: Cut the kidney into thin slices, cook as the liver. A tablespoon tomato ketchup and a few drops Worcestershire sauce can be added to the stock, or water and stock cube.

Gourmet Touch: **Braised Liver Niçoise:** Use sliced calves' or lambs' liver and increase the tomatoes to 4–6. Slice the liver thickly but chop the onions finely and cook for 3 minutes only at H/15 lb pressure. A little red wine could be used instead of all stock, or water and stock cube.

Braised Liver Lyonnaise: Omit the tomatoes; use 4 thickly sliced potatoes and 4 onions instead, and half white wine and half stock.

BRAISED PIGEONS

Braising is an ideal way to cook pigeons or, indeed, any game. The cooking time should be adjusted according to the age of the birds.

Serves 4
Pressure cooking time 15–20 mins

---

4 small pigeons
Salt and pepper

FOR THE MIREPOIX:
1 thick slice bacon
3 onions
2–3 sticks celery
3–4 tomatoes
25–40 g (1–1½ oz) dripping or fat (optional)
Good 280 ml (½ pt) brown stock or water
Bouquet garni (see page 16) or pinch dried herbs
Small piece cabbage (optional)
140 ml (¼ pt) red wine
15 g (½ oz) flour

TO GARNISH:
4 large slices toast

---

1 Wash and dry the pigeons and season.
2 Dice the bacon, keep the rind, and slice the vegetables.
3 Heat the bacon and bacon rind in the pressure cooker and fry the

pigeons with the sliced onions until golden. If the bacon does not produce enough fat, use the 25–40 g (1–1½ oz) dripping or fat too.

4   Lift the pigeons out of the pan, add the rest of the vegetables, stock or water and herbs, and season lightly.

5   Replace the pigeons, fix the cover, bring up to H/15 lb pressure and cook for 15–20 minutes according to the age of the birds.

6   Reduce pressure under cold water; lift the pigeons on to a hot dish.

7   Shred the cabbage very finely, then add to the vegetables in the pan and cook without pressure for 1 minute.

8   Blend the wine and flour together, stir into the vegetable mixture and stir the mixture over a low heat until thickened.

9   Cut the toast into triangles, arrange round the edge of the dish and spoon the wine sauce over or round the pigeons.

TO VARY:

The vegetable mixture may be sieved or emulsified and flavoured with a little white wine and served as a sauce, without thickening with the flour.

Braised Pheasants: Follow the directions for cooking pigeons. If cooking a young pheasant keep this whole and allow about 10 minutes pressure cooking. A large plump young pheasant will serve 3–4. Older birds could be jointed and may need 15–20 minutes cooking.

Gourmet Touch: Braising is a gourmet method of cooking, so any braised game is suitable for a special party. It could be prepared ahead and just warmed through at the last minute in the cooker (using this as an ordinary pan). The garnish can be varied to add interest, e.g. garnish with canned Morello cherries using a little of the syrup in the mirepoix, or garnish with small Frankfurter sausages.

BASED ON BRAISED PIGEONS

Braised Beef: Allow a thick slice topside per person; cook for 15 minutes at H/15 lb (stage 5). Or you could buy a joint of topside or brisket, calculate the cooking time at 12–15 minutes per 450 g (1 lb).

Braised Lambs' Kidneys: Allow 4 lambs' kidneys per person. Cook for 5 minutes at H/15 lb (stage 5).

Braised Sweetbreads: First blanch the sweetbreads by putting into the open cooker with cold water to cover. Bring the water slowly to the boil, strain the sweetbreads, dry thoroughly. Remove any pieces of gristle with kitchen scissors; discard the water. Cook the sweetbreads for 6 minutes at H/15 lb (stage 5).

Braised Oxtail: Cut into portions. Allow from 25–40 minutes (see page 79-80) at H/15 lb (stage 5).

Braised Chicken: Use jointed chicken instead of pigeon. If young, allow 5 minutes; if a boiling fowl, 8–10 minutes at H/15 lb (stage 5).

TO BOIL MEAT AND POULTRY

Boiling is a process used for many meats – beef, ham, bacon, tongue, etc., as well as for chicken, and special ways of dealing with each meat are described in the recipes that follow.

Fresh meat: Allow about 170 g (6 oz) meat per person (weight without bone) before cooking. There is no need to soak this before cooking. Season with salt and pepper in the usual way.

Salted meats: These shrink more in the process of cooking so allow about 225 g (8 oz) meat per person (weight without bone) before cooking. Salted meats should be soaked in cold water to cover for some hours, preferably overnight; or you can put the meat into the pressure cooker with water to cover; bring the water slowly to the boil, allow the meat to stand in the water for 5 minutes, and then throw the water away. This saves time in soaking and is very suitable for *lightly* salted meats. Do not add salt when cooking salted meats, just pepper to season. Herbs and vegetables are generally added.

Timing: The time is given in each recipe per 450 g (1 lb). If cooking a very small joint of only about 450 g (1 lb) in total weight then allow an extra 5 minutes. The different time depends upon the thickness of the joint; a long thin joint cooks rather more quickly than a small thick one.

Trivet: Do not use the trivet, for the food should be covered with liquid.

Liquid: Make sure that sufficient water, or other liquid, is placed in the cooker to cover the meat, but do not fill the cooker more than half full when both meat and water are placed in the pan. Cider is a very pleasant liquid to use when boiling bacon, see the particular recipe.

Pressure: Bring rapidly to H/15 lb pressure, lower heat and time the cooking. You may need to reduce pressure to add vegetables and the method of doing this is given in the recipe. You then bring once again to H/15 lb pressure and continue cooking.

Reducing pressure: Reduce pressure under cold water if serving the meat hot, but allow to cool at room temperature and leave in the liquid if serving the meat cold, in which case deduct 2–3 minutes from the total pressure cooking time.

Note: The stock has a better colour if you bring the liquid to the boil and then remove any scum before fixing the cover; this is particularly effective when the meat has a fair percentage of fat.

BOILED BACON AND HAM

There are many joints that can be chosen for boiling. The cheaper collar, forehock, hock, become very tender if cooked under pressure. For special occasions use gammon or prepared ham, or long back bacon.

There are various methods of curing bacon today; if salted follow the advice given above under **Salted meats**. If unsalted, often called 'green bacon' or 'sweetcure', then there is no need to soak.

Allow 7–8 minutes per 450 g (1 lb) for the prime joints or 12 minutes per 450 g (1 lb) at H/15 lb pressure for the cheaper cuts. Cider, ginger ale, and pineapple juice are all good flavourings with bacon, mix them with water or use instead of water.

The step-by-step method of cooking the meat is similar to salt beef, below. If the bacon is very fat, it is better to stand in on the trivet so the fat can run out into the liquid.

TO VARY:

Glazed Bacon: Deduct about 5 minutes from the total pressure cooking time. Remove the rind from the bacon, score the fat, then press brown sugar, blended with a little made mustard and fruit juice, over the fat and brown for 20 minutes, or until tender, in the centre of a moderate to moderately hot oven, 190–200°C (375–400°F), Gas Mark 5–6. This may be served hot or cold.

BOILED SALT BEEF

Serves see page 88
Pressure cooking time 12–15 mins per 450 g (1 lb)

1–1½ kg (2–3 lb) salt brisket or silverside of beef
Carrots, onions, turnips, etc.
Pepper

TO GARNISH
chopped parsley

---

1   Prepare the salted meat as on page 88.
2   Peel the vegetables, dice if large.

3 Put the meat into the cooker, add water to half-fill pan, a shake of pepper and 1 onion, 1 carrot to flavour the meat and stock during cooking.

4 Fix the cover, bring to H/15 lb pressure; lower the heat and time the cooking; allow the slightly shorter time for very good quality silverside. Deduct 5 minutes from the total time if serving the meat hot.

5 Reduce the pressure under cold water 5 minutes before the end of the cooking time, add the vegetables and bring again to H/15 lb pressure.

6 Cook for 5 minutes, reduce the pressure under cold water.

7 Serve the meat garnished with the whole vegetables and chopped parsley and with some of the unthickened stock as a gravy.

TO VARY:

If you plan to serve the joint cold, reduce pressure, but keep meat, etc., in the pan and allow it to cool in the stock, then remove, wrap and store. The cold meat will then be more moist.

Boiled Salt Beef and Dumplings: Make the dumplings as on page 100. Add to the liquid after stage 6 (see page 101), then serve with the vegetables. A mustard dumpling is excellent with boiled salt beef.

Gourmet Touch: **Glazed Salt Beef:** This makes an excellent buffet party dish. Omit most of the vegetables, but add sufficient, and a bouquet garni, to flavour the stock. Cook to stage 4, allow full time. Lift meat from stock, reduce the liquid and continue as in the glazed tongue recipe.

TO COOK OX TONGUE

Serves see page 88
Pressure cooking time 15 mins per 450 g (1 lb)

---

1 ox tongue
Carrots, onions, turnips, etc.
Pepper, salt (if necessary)
Bouquet garni (see page 16) (if necessary)
15 g (½ oz) gelatine (if serving cold)

---

1 If the tongue is salted, prepare as given on page 88 (under **Salted meats**). If you intend to cook the tongue to serve cold, then use only 1 onion, 1 carrot and a small bouquet garni.

2 Follow stages 3 and 4 under salt beef.

3 Reduce the pressure; if serving cold, cool slightly, then remove from the cooker, skin and take out any bones.

4   If serving hot: use the stock to make a sauce.

If serving cold; make a glaze by boiling the stock in the open pan until about 280 ml (½ pt) remains, dissolve the gelatine in this.

Roll the tongue to make a tight fit in a round casserole, tin or a saucepan, then strain the gelatine stock over the top.

Place a plate and light weight over the tongue, leave until set, and lift away any fat that rises to the top of the jelly once it has set.

TO VARY:

Lambs' Tongues: These are ideal for small families. Cook as above, allow 15–20 minutes at H/15 lb pressure.

Gourmet Touch: **Tongue in Madeira Sauce:** Either prepare the sauce as on page 104, or make a sweeter sauce as follows. To serve 6–8: blend 1 level tablespoon arrowroot or cornflour with 280 ml (½ pt) carefully strained stock from the pressure cooker and 280 ml (½ pt) Madeira wine. Put into a saucepan with 2 tablespoons redcurrant jelly and seasoning to taste. Stir over a low heat until thickened and clear.

Tongue in Walnut Mayonnaise: A delicious sauce with cold tongue is made by adding finely chopped, skinned walnuts to mayonnaise.

BOILED CHICKEN

A boiled chicken is an excellent basis for a number of dishes, or an ideal way of cooking a chicken if you want to make sandwiches.

Serves 3–4
Pressure cooking time 5–10 mins per 450 g (1 lb), see stage 4

Boiling fowl or chicken, approximately 1½ kg (3 lb)
Salt and pepper
25 g (1 oz) butter (optional)
280–560 ml (½–1 pt) water*
2–3 sticks celery
2 small onions
Bouquet garni (see page 16) or pinch mixed dried herbs

---

1   Wash and dry the bird, season lightly. Spread the butter over the breast of a young chicken.

2   Put all the ingredients into the pressure cooker, do not use the trivet.

3   Fix the cover and bring to H/15 lb pressure.

4   Lower the heat, time the cooking: allow only 5 minutes per 450 g (1 lb) for young chickens, but 10 minutes per 450 g (1 lb) for an older boiling fowl is necessary.

5   Reduce the pressure under cold water.

*   If the chicken stock is required for sauces, etc. (see below), use the larger quantity of water.

TO VARY:

Chicken Supreme: Strain off 280 ml (½ pt) of the chicken stock. Heat 40 g (1½ oz) butter in a pan, stir in 40 g (1½ oz) flour, blend in 140 ml (¼ pt) milk and the stock. Bring to the boil, stir until thickened. Whisk the yolks of 2 eggs and 2–3 tablespoons double cream together, whisk into the hot, but not boiling, sauce. Cook gently for 2–3 minutes. Carve breast meat and coat with the sauce. Serve with boiled rice (page 120). Garnish with chopped hard-boiled egg and parsley.

Chicken Velouté: Follow recipe for Chicken Supreme, use all chicken stock and omit the milk. Add 2 tablespoons dry sherry to the egg yolks and cream and cook as above.

CHAUDFROID OF CHICKEN

Prepare the chicken as in the recipe above.

Measure 280 ml (½ pt) chicken stock, strain carefully.

Dissolve half a packet of aspic jelly plus 1 teaspoon gelatine in stock and allow to cool. Blend with 3 tablespoons mayonnaise and 140 ml (¼ pt) double cream. Cut the chicken into convenient joints, carefully cut away the bones, but keep the shape intact.

Coat with the half-set aspic mixture. Garnish with small pieces of gherkin, cucumber, tomato, and leave to set.

BOILED LAMB WITH CAPER SAUCE

Although you can use economical pieces of lamb (or mutton) as chosen for the Irish Stew and other recipes on page 74-75, this dish is ideal for a special occasion when made with half a leg of lamb.

Serves 6
Pressure cooking time 10–11 mins per 450 g (1 lb)

½ large leg of lamb
Carrots, onions, turnips, etc.
Salt and pepper

FOR THE SAUCE:
40 g (1½ oz) butter or margarine
40 g (1½ oz) flour
280 ml (½ pt) lamb stock
140 ml (¼ pt) milk
2–3 teaspoons capers
Little vinegar

TO GARNISH:
chopped parsley

1   Put the lamb into the cooker.

2   Prepare the vegetables, then follow directions for Salt Beef on page 89.

3   Strain off 280 ml (½ pt) stock; heat the butter or margarine in a pan, stir in the flour, blend in the stock and milk.

4   Bring to the boil, cook until thickened, *then* add the capers and a little vinegar from the jar of capers, season well.

5   Carve the lamb and coat with the sauce, top with parsley.

COLD DISHES

Roasted meats, pages 95 and 97, will often be served cold, but the following recipes are for cold moulds.

BRAWN

Serves 6–8
Pressure cooking time 30–35 mins

½ lamb's, pig's or calf's head
Generous 1 litre (1¾ pt) water
2 carrots
2 onions
Salt and pepper
Bouquet garni (see page 16)
Strip lemon rind
Gelatine – see stage 5

1   Soak the head in cold water, place in the cooker, and cover with water, bring steadily to the boil, discard the water; this ensures a clear jelly.

2   Replace the head in the cooker with 1 litre (1¼ pt) fresh water, peeled whole vegetables and the rest of the ingredients, except the gelatine.

3   Fix the cover, bring to H/15 lb pressure, lower the heat; cook for 30 minutes (for the smaller lamb's head) and 35 minutes for the larger heads.

4   Reduce pressure, remove head from stock, cool, cut away all the meat from the bones; replace the bones in the stock and boil in the open cooker until approximately 280 ml (½ pt) remains; strain, return to the cooker.

5   If using calf's head there is sufficient natural gelatine, but it is advisable to dissolve 1 teaspoon gelatine in the stock when using pig's or lamb's head, to set the brawn firmly.

6   Dice the meat, return to the stock and warm through, then spoon into an oiled basin or mould and leave to set.

TO VARY:

Chicken and Lemon Brawn: Cook a small chicken with juice of 1 lemon and ingredients as above for 10 minutes at H/15 lb. Dice flesh, proceed as above.

BEEF GALANTINE

Serves 6–8
Pressure cooking time 35 mins

---

50 g (2 oz) breadcrumbs
4 tablespoons beef stock
450 g (1 lb) good quality stewing steak or topside of beef
100–170 g (4–6 oz) bacon
225 g (8 oz) sausage meat
2 eggs
Salt and pepper
½ teaspoon fresh sage or good pinch dried sage

---

1   Put the crumbs into a large basin, add the stock and leave for 15 minutes to soften.

2   Put the beef and bacon through a mincer, add to the crumbs with

the rest of the ingredients.

3 Press into a well-greased 1-kg (2-lb) dish or tin, cover with a double thickness of greased greaseproof paper.

4 Place the trivet and 420 ml (¾ pt) water into the cooker, add a little vinegar, as suggested for steamed puddings, page 125.

5 Bring to H/15 lb pressure, cook for 35 minutes, reduce pressure (unless using an ovenproof glass dish when it is advisable to let the pressure drop gradually, in which case allow 32 minutes at H/15 lb).

6 Remove damp covers, place dry paper and a light weight on top, allow to cool.

TO VARY:

Chicken Galantine: Mince raw chicken and use in place of beef in the recipe above.

Gourmet Touch: **Terrine of Chicken or Game:** Cut the flesh from a 1–1½ kg (2–3 lb) chicken or game bird(s). Mince the leg and back meat with 170 g (6 oz) bacon and the liver of the bird(s). Blend with 225 g (8 oz) sausage meat, 1 egg, 4 tablespoons stock, sherry or brandy. Season and flavour with ½ teaspoon chopped lemon thyme. Slice the breast meat neatly. Put layers of minced mixture and sliced breast into the container, beginning and ending with the minced mixture. Cover and cook as in the recipe above.

TO ROAST MEAT, POULTRY AND GAME

Many people consider that the only true roasting is done over a fire with the food turning on a spit. We now associate the roasting process with cooking in the oven. But people often overlook the advantages of pot roasting which can be done so quickly and successfully in a pressure cooker.

Pot roasting has advantages over other methods of roasting:

a) The food is first browned, and so looks delicious. Then a small amount of liquid is added, and the steam from this helps to tenderize the meat, poultry or game, and also keeps it moist.

b) It is very simple to cook vegetables with the meat, so you can prepare the entire main course in one container. The vegetables have a good flavour and they also give flavour to the liquid in the bottom of the cooker.

c) While one can pot roast prime cuts of meat or very tender poultry or game, another great advantage is that the less tender joints, which might give disappointing results if roasted in the oven, give extremely good results from the pressure cooker.

A PERFECT POT ROAST

Selecting the meat: Choose a joint or bird that does not exceed 1½ kg (3 lb). Always weigh the meat or bird when the stuffing has been added, to give the total weight. Follow the time table on page 97.

Browning the meat: Wipe the meat to absorb surface moisture and so minimize splashing in the base of the cooker. Dust with lightly seasoned flour (this helps to give good browning). Add any other flavouring, as suggested on page 98. Remove the trivet. Heat 25–50 g (1–2 oz) fat or well-clarified dripping (see page 98) in the bottom of the cooker.

The amount of fat depends upon whether the joint is very lean or has some natural fat.

Brown the joint all over, turning it with the help of large spoons.

Remove the joint from the cooker when it is really brown. If there is rather a lot of fat left in the base of the cooker, remove the cooker from the heat and spoon, or strain, the surplus fat from the cooker – use this for dripping.

Liquid: Pour 560 ml (1 pt) boiling water, or stock or other liquid, into the cooker, stir very well to absorb any brown residue at the base of the pan.

Trivet: This is removed when browning the meat, but returned to the cooker at this stage. Place the meat on the trivet.

Pressure: Fix the cover, bring up to H/15 lb pressure, lower the heat and cook for time given in the table on page 97.

Reducing pressure: Reduce the pressure 5 minutes before the end of the total cooking time; do this under cold water. Add the vegetables round the meat, bring to pressure again and complete the cooking.

To serve: Lift the joint and vegetables on to a hot dish. Remove the trivet and make the gravy with the liquid in the cooker.

TO MAKE GRAVY

The liquid in the base of the cooker contains the meat juices that have dripped down during cooking, so makes excellent gravy.

For a thin gravy: Blend 1–1½ tablespoons flour with 2–3 table-spoons cold water; stir into the hot liquid in the cooker. Stir to whisk over a medium heat as this thickens. Strain into the sauce boat.

For a thick gravy: Use double the amount of flour.

TIME TABLE FOR ROASTING

MEAT	TIMING	SERVE WITH:
Bacon or ham:		
Most cuts	see page 89	see page 102
Beef:		
Prime cuts – sirloin or rib	9-10 minutes per 450 g (1lb)	Horseradish sauce, page 108, or mustard
Cheaper cuts – topside or rump	12-15 minutes per 450 g (1lb)	
Lamb or Mutton:		
Prime cuts – half leg or loin or best end of neck	10-11 minutes per 450 g (1lb)	Mint sauce, page 108, or Onion sauce, page 108 or redcurrant jelly
Cheaper cuts – breast (boned and rolled), leg of mutton, middle neck	12-14 minutes per 450 g (1lb)	
Pork:		
Must be very lean and only prime cuts are likely to be – thick fillet from leg	13-15 minutes per 450 g (1lb)	Sage and onion stuffing, page 101, Apple sauce page 105
Veal:		
Prime cuts – loin, thick fillet from leg	10-12 minutes per 450 g (1lb)	Veal stuffing page 102. Bread sauce, page 108
Cheaper cuts – best end of neck, rolled breast	12-14 minutes per 450 g (1lb)	
Poultry:		
Chicken	5 minutes per 450 g (1 lb)	As veal
Duckling	ditto	As pork or see below
Part of turkey	ditto	As veal or see below
Young game –		
grouse, *pheasant, pigeon*	5 minutes per 450 g (1 lb)	See below
Saddle of leveret (young hare)	8-10 minutes per 450 g (1 lb)	Sage and onion stuffing, page 101
Venison	12–14 minutes per 450 g (1 lb)	Sage and onion stuffing, page 101

GIVING FLAVOUR TO THE JOINT

Bacon: Sweetcure bacon is good if roasted; add a little brown sugar to the flour and/or a good pinch ground ginger or finely grated lemon rind.

Beef: Flavour flour with mustard powder.

Lamb: Add finely chopped rosemary to the flour or make small slits in the skin of the lamb. Peel and slice a clove of garlic and insert slivers into the slits.

Pork: As bacon.

Veal: Cut very narrow strips of fat bacon, insert in the lean flesh (this is called 'larding') with a larding needle.

Chicken or Turkey: If this is not being stuffed, flavour the flour with chopped rosemary or grated lemon rind (add a little lemon juice to the stock or water).

Duckling: If you are not making stuffing, put sliced apples and/or soaked, but not cooked, prunes inside or add a little red wine to the stock or water.

Game: Excellent if a little cream cheese and deseeded, skinned grapes are put into game birds. Use beer with stock for venison.

Dripping adds flavour to all meats. Clean this by heating gently with water. Cool, then take the clarified dripping from the top of the water, remove any tiny particles of food from the underside.

STEAK AND KIDNEY PUDDING

There are two ways in which you can prepare this pudding. The time for pressure cooking will vary and is given in stage 7. You can also freeze the pudding in various ways.

You can:

a) Pre-cook the meat, as on page 70-71 (for steak and kidney pie), but allow only 10 minutes at H/15 lb and do not over-thicken the gravy. Cook as stage 7 a).

To freeze: prepare, but do not cook. Defrost for some hours, then cook as stage 7 a).

b) Use raw meat and pressure cook as 7 b). If freezing shorten cooking time by 10 minutes at L/5 lb. To reheat, defrost then allow 30 minutes at L/5 lb.

c) For freezing: prepare pudding with raw meat, freeze. Defrost then cook as 7 b).

Serves 6–8
Steaming time 15 mins
Pressure cooking time a) 25 mins
b) 55 mins

FOR THE PASTRY:

170–225 g (6–8 oz) self-raising flour (or plain flour and 1½–2 teaspoons
baking powder)*
Pinch salt
75–100 g (3–4 oz)* shredded suet
Water to mix

FOR THE FILLING:

450 g (1 lb) stewing steak
100–170 g (4–6 oz) ox kidneys or 2–3 lambs' kidneys
Salt and pepper
1 tablespoon flour
Little stock or water

---

1   Prepare the suet crust as for the dumplings, page 100, but make
the dough to a soft rolling consistency.
   *The varying amounts of flour and suet are for a thin or rather
thick layer of pastry. If you like the pastry very thin, use plain flour
and no raising agent.

2   Roll out the pastry on a floured board and take approximately
two-thirds to line a lightly greased basin.

3   With cooked meat spoon into suet crust pastry.
   With raw meat: dice the steak and kidney, coat in seasoned flour,
put into the pastry-lined basin with liquid to come two-thirds of the
way up the basin.

4   Damp the edges of the pastry, roll the remaining dough into a
round, press on top of the filling, seal the edges firmly. Cover with
greased greaseproof paper or foil.

5   Stand the trivet in the pressure cooker, add ¾ litre (1¼ pt) boiling
water for the shorter pressure cooking time or generous ¾ litre (1½
pt) for the longer cooking time. Add a little vinegar or lemon juice
(see page 125).

6   Make a string handle or foil band, as suggested on page 125, and
lower the pudding into the cooker.

7   Steam for 15 minutes, then bring steadily to L/5 lb pressure,

lower the heat and:

    a) cook for 25 minutes;
    b) cook for 55 minutes.

8   Allow pressure to drop at room temperature.

9   Serve the pudding with a thickened gravy or more clear stock.

TO VARY:

Cornish Pudding: Use the diced steak, but replace the kidney with diced onion. Add 2 diced potatoes and do not flour the meat.

Kentish Chicken Pudding: Use diced raw chicken and diced root vegetables instead of steak and kidney. Flavour the seasoned flour with a little chopped parsley and/or chopped chives. Make a stock from the bones.

Rabbit Pudding: Use diced raw rabbit and diced inexpensive streaky bacon instead of steak and kidney. Flavour the seasoned flour with ½–1 teaspoon chopped fresh sage or a good pinch dried sage. Make stock from the bones.

Vegetable Pudding: Use a good mixture of diced root vegetables, onions and peas or beans to give protein. The pressure cooking time can be shortened to 25 minutes at L/5 lb. Before serving, lift the suet pastry lid and add a good sprinkling of grated cheese to the vegetables.

DUMPLINGS FOR STEWS AND BOILED MEATS

It is better to cook dumplings without pressure, since they take only between 7 and 12 minutes to cook, see stage 6 below.

Serves 4–8 depending upon the dish
Cooking time 7–12 mins (no pressure used)

---

100 g (4 oz) self-raising flour (or plain flour and 1 teaspoon baking powder)
Salt
25–50 g (1–2 oz) shredded suet or margarine or cooking fat
Water to mix

---

1   Sieve the flour, or flour and baking powder, with the salt.

2   Add the suet, or rub in the margarine or fat.

3   Mix with enough cold water to make a slightly sticky mixture.

4   Roll into small balls with floured hands to required size.

5   When the food in the cooker is tender and the pressure at zero,

remove the cover. Check there is adequate liquid (dumplings absorb a lot), thicken if desired, bring to the boil.

6   Drop in the dumplings. Lay the cover on top of the pressure cooker, but *do not fix it*, or use a plate if preferred. The cooker then becomes an ordinary saucepan. Cook steadily until well-risen (time depends on size).

TO VARY:

Herb Dumplings: Add 2 tablespoons chopped herbs (parsley, chives, sage, thyme, etc.) to the flour, etc.

Horseradish Dumplings: Add 1–2 teaspoons grated horseradish or 1–2 tablespoons horseradish cream to flour.

Mustard Dumplings: Sieve ½–1 teaspoon mustard powder with the flour.

Onion Dumplings: Add 2–3 teaspoons grated onion to the flour, etc.

Note: Add all flavourings before binding the flour, etc., with water.

Gourmet Touch: **Golden Dumplings:** Rub 50 g (2 oz) butter into the flour. Bind with 1 egg and a very little water. These are delicious cooked in consommé (see page 27).

STUFFINGS

SAGE AND ONION STUFFING

Serves 4–6
Pressure cooking time 1 min and as main dish

1   Peel and chop 2 large onions, put into the cooker with 140 ml (¼ pt) water and seasoning.

2   Bring to H/15 lb pressure and cook for 1 minute.

3   Reduce pressure, strain the onions, blend with 100 g (4 oz) shredded suet or melted margarine, 2 teaspoons chopped fresh sage or ½–1 teaspoon dried sage, salt and pepper.

4   Bind with a little stock or you may prefer to use an egg.

Use this stuffing in poultry (duck and goose), pork, etc.

VEAL (PARSLEY AND LEMON) STUFFING

Serves 4–6
Pressure cooking time as main dish

1   Grate the top zest (the yellow part of the rind) from 1 lemon and squeeze out some or all of the juice.

2   Add the lemon rind to 100 g (4 oz) soft breadcrumbs, add 1–2 teaspoons chopped, fresh or ½ teaspoon dried mixed herbs, 50 g (2 oz) shredded suet, or melted margarine, salt and pepper and 1 egg.

3   Stir in sufficient lemon juice to give the desired flavour.

Use this stuffing in poultry, meat and fish dishes.

TO VARY:

The crumbs and herbs may be chopped in the blender, together with thin strips of lemon zest.

Giblet Stuffing: Add the finely chopped raw, or lightly cooked, liver of poultry to the other ingredients.

Rice Stuffings: Use cooked rice in place of breadcrumbs in either the sage and onion of veal stuffing.

MAKING SAUCES

The following sauces, made in minutes, can transform cooked meats or poultry. It would be practical, if you have a freezer, to make larger quantities. Wine loses a little potency in freezing so add extra when reheating.

The basic sauce to serve with meat dishes is a Brown Sauce; melt 25 g (1 oz) fat in the pan, stir in 25 g (1 oz) flour, add 280 ml (½ pt) brown stock (see page 25). Stir over a low heat until thickened and smooth, season to taste.

To make a sauce with more flavour, fry a finely chopped onion and carrot in the fat first then proceed as for the basic sauce.

CUMBERLAND SAUCE

This sauce is served cold with ham or pâtés, but can be an excellent way to heat cooked ham.

Serves 4–6
Pressure cooking time 5 mins

2 large oranges
2 small or 1 large lemon
280 ml (½ pt) white stock or water
1½ teaspoons arrowroot or cornflour
1 teaspoon made English mustard
4 tablespoons port wine
6 tablespoons redcurrant jelly
Salt and pepper

1   Cut the top rind (zest) from the fruit; do not use the white pith. Cut the zest into thin matchsticks and put into the cooker with the stock or water.

2   Bring to H/15 lb pressure, cook for 5 minutes, reduce the pressure and remove the cover.

3   Squeeze the juice from the fruit, blend with the arrowroot or cornflour, then with the liquid in the cooker, add the other ingredients and stir over a low heat until thickened and clear.

TO VARY:

Orange Sauce: Omit the lemon and mustard, use stock obtained from cooking duck giblets and only 2–3 tablespoons jelly. Serve with duckling.

ESPAGNOLE SAUCE

This is a classic sauce that is ideal to serve with meats, poultry, etc. It is very good with roasted bacon.

Serves 5
Pressure cooking time 8 mins

1 small onion
1 small carrot
2 medium tomatoes
2 medium mushrooms
1 rasher bacon
25 g (1 oz) dripping or margarine
280 ml (½ pt) brown stock
Bouquet garni (see page 16)

Salt and pepper
25 g (1 oz) flour
3 tablespoons dry sherry

1   Peel and chop the vegetables; there is no need to peel the mushrooms or dice the vegetables carefully, unless the sauce is not to be sieved or emulsified.

2   Remove the rind from the bacon and dice the rasher finely if you do not intend to sieve or liquidise the sauce.

3   Heat the dripping or margarine in the open pressure pan and fry the bacon and vegetables for a few minutes.

4   Add the stock, the bouquet garni and seasoning.

5   Fix the cover, bring to H/15 lb pressure and cook for 8 minutes.

6   Allow pressure to drop then remove the cover.

7   Blend the flour with the sherry, stir into the pan and cook until thickened; remove bacon rind and bouquet garni.

8   It is usual, but not essential, to sieve or liquidise this sauce.

9   Serve the sauce over jointed boiled chicken, sliced, cooked meat or poached fish.

TO VARY:

Madeira Sauce: use half stock and half Madeira wine in making the sauce, then blend the flour with Madeira. This sauce is excellent over sliced cooked tongue or ham or poultry, see also page 91.

Pepper Sauce: Add a teaspoon crushed peppercorns (tied in muslin).

BOLOGNESE SAUCE

This is the classic meat sauce served with spaghetti or other pasta dishes.

Serves 4–6
Pressure cooking time 5–6 mins

1 small green pepper (optional)
1 medium onion
1 medium carrot
3 medium tomatoes
50 g (2 oz) mushrooms
1 clove garlic (optional)
25 g (1 oz) butter

1 tablespoon olive oil
140 ml (¼ pt) brown stock
140 ml (¼ pt) red wine
170–225 g (6–8 oz) minced beef
Salt and pepper

1 Dice the pepper (discard core and seeds), peel and dice the onion and carrot, skin and chop the tomatoes, wipe and slice the mushrooms. Crush the garlic.

2 Heat the butter and oil in the cooker, fry the vegetables gently for several minutes.

3 Add stock, wine, meat and seasoning then continue as Savoury Mince, page 73, but do not thicken the sauce with flour. Reduce the pressure, remove the cover and allow the sauce to simmer for 5–10 minutes until the liquid is reduced.

FRUIT SAUCES

Apple sauce is excellent with pork, duck and goose. Cranberry sauce has become a popular accompaniment to turkey.

Apple Sauce: Make the sauce as the purée on page 142, add a little knob of butter to the cooked purée.

Cranberry Sauce: Make the sauce as the purée on page 142. You can use a little port wine instead of all water, or half orange juice and half water. When the purée is cooked, add 1–2 tablespoons redcurrant jelly to give a sweeter taste.

TOMATO SAUCE

This sauce can be served with spaghetti or other pasta dishes. It is an excellent sauce to serve with meat, fish or poultry dishes, or over some vegetables.

Serves 4–6
Pressure cooking time 5 mins

450 g (1 lb) tomatoes
1 onion
1 small dessert apple (optional)
1 rasher streaky bacon (optional)

25 g (1 oz) butter or margarine
280 ml (½ pt) white stock or water
Salt and pepper
1 teaspoon brown sugar
2 teaspoons cornflour

---

1   Skin the tomatoes and chop, then peel and chop the onion, remove the core and chop the apple.

2   Remove the bacon rind and chop the rasher of bacon.

3   Put all the ingredients, except the cornflour, into the cooker.

4   Bring to H/15 lb and cook for 5 minutes, reduce the pressure and remove the cover; take out the bacon rind.

5   Sieve or liquidise the ingredients, then tip back into the cooker.

6   Blend the cornflour with a little water, stir into the purée and stir over a low heat until thickened.

TO VARY:

It you do not want to sieve or liquidise the tomato mixture, then grate the onion and apple or chop finely, and cut the bacon into very small pieces.

You can give extra flavour to the sauce by adding a bay leaf; small sprig basil and/or parsley; by adding a crushed clove garlic, or a few drops soy or Worcestershire sauce.

If you like a richer texture then toss the onion and apple in 25 g (1 oz) butter before adding the liquid.

A tablespoon tomato purée (from a tube or can) gives a stronger taste and adds 'bite' to the sauce. Use a large (400 g) can of tomatoes (the plum type are good) when fresh tomatoes are expensive, with liquid from the can plus stock or water to give 280 ml (½ pt).

WEEKEND SPECIALS

Most people enjoy their leisure time during the weekend, and the suggestions on this page are for easy, but interesting, meals which are planned to take the minimum of time and effort. All the ideas are based upon recipes or cooking processes given in detail in other parts of the book, and the page numbers to which you should refer are given.

The timing by each recipe title is for pressure cooking at H/15 lb. Where quantities are given they are for 4 people.

In some cases you may well be able to cook fruit in a container with the main course, to have for dessert.

KEDGEREE

5 mins

Put 280 ml (½ pt) water in the cooker, carefully put 3 eggs in the water, add a whole peeled onion if desired, season lightly. Place 175 g (6 oz) long grain rice, 420 ml (¾ pt) water and little salt into a solid container, stand in the cooker, cover with greased paper (see page 120). Lay the trivet over this, and put a smoked haddock on the trivet. Bring to H/15 lb pressure, allow pressure to drop after the 5 minutes cooking. Flake the fish, chop 2 eggs, slice third egg, chop the onion. Drain the rice, rinse if desired. Blend the rice, fish, egg white and onion in the open cooker, moisten with a little cream. Add pepper to taste, then spoon on to a hot dish and top with chopped egg yolks, sliced egg and parsley.

To make the meal more substantial, the separator could be filled with diced vegetables which should be cooked with the fish, etc.

TURBOT HOLLANDAISE

5 mins

Follow directions for kedgeree, using seasoned slices of turbot instead of haddock. Blend the rinsed rice with chopped hardboiled eggs, chopped onion and a little cream. Arrange on a dish, top with the fish and **Hollandaise sauce**. To make the sauce: put 2 egg yolks, a pinch salt, pepper and mustard with 1–2 tablespoons lemon juice into a basin. Whisk over hot water until thick, then gradually whisk in 50 g (2 oz) softened butter.

HERBED CHICKEN

5 mins

Fry 4 portions of young chicken in 50 g (2 oz) butter in the open cooker. Remove, and fill the base of the cooker with sliced onions, sliced tomatoes plus seasoning and 280 ml (½ pt) stock or water. Place the trivet in the cooker, cover the chicken with chopped fresh herbs, cook as for braising (page 83). Serve with **Bread sauce**. To make the sauce; put 100 g (4 oz) soft crumbs, a peeled onion, 280 ml (½ pt) milk, 25 g (1 oz) butter and seasoning into a pan, bring to the boil, then allow to stand for a time. Remove the onion, heat sauce gently, and then serve.

TO VARY:

Herbed Lamb 12 mins
Use thick loin chops instead of the chicken. Serve with **Mint sauce**. To make the sauce: chop young mint leaves and flavour with sugar and vinegar.

Herbed Mutton 15 mins
Use thick mutton chops instead of chicken. Serve with **Onion sauce**. Cook the onions, etc., under the trivet as in Herbed Chicken; also cook a peeled whole onion on the trivet for Onion sauce. Chop the cooked onion, blend with white sauce, as on page 53.

Savoury Beef 10 mins
Cook 4 thick slices of topside as described under Herbed Chicken. Serve with **Horseradish sauce**. To make the sauce: blend grated fresh horseradish, a little made mustard, sugar, salt and pepper and lemon juice with double cream or white sauce (page 53).

Note: Cook suitable vegetables in the separator with the main dish (see page 68 and 100–115).

CURRIES

From 8 mins

Peel and chop 1 onion and 1 dessert apple. Fry in 50 g (2 oz) butter in the open cooker, add 1–2 tablespoons curry powder, then add 280–420 ml (½–¾ pt) stock, plus a few sultanas, little grated coconut, chutney, seasoning, sugar and lemon juice to taste. Add enough diced raw chicken or cooked meat for 4, bring to pressure and cook for 3 minutes.

Reduce pressure, place the trivet over the curry and add the rice in a container (described on page 120). Bring once again to pressure and complete the cooking. The sauce can be thickened at the end if wished.

COOKING VEGETABLES

Over the years we have learned the importance of cooking vegetables correctly. It is not surprising that we all try to follow the 'conserved method' of cooking vegetables to retain the maximum flavour, colour, firm texture and vitamin content.

If you consider how vegetables are cooked under pressure, i.e. in the minimum quantity of liquid for the shortest period of cooking, you will realize why they taste so good.

POINTS TO REMEMBER

Preparation of vegetables: Peel, scrape or wash and shred or chop as though cooking by any other method. Make sure that the vegetables are all of the same size, to ensure even cooking. See stage 1, regarding the preparation of green vegetables. If you intend cooking a selection of different vegetables in the cooker then cut them into the right sizes so they will all be cooked to perfection at the same time, i.e. halve or quarter potatoes, chop carrots, etc., if cooking these with green vegetables.

Seasoning: Most of us like to cook vegetables in salted water, but as you will use so little water in the pressure cooker, and as the vegetables retain more of their own mineral salts in the rapid cooking, be a little more sparing with salt than usual.

Timing: This is particularly important when cooking vegetables. The recipes and information in this chapter give the average timing required; do not exceed this. It is very simple to cool the cooker and check the vegetables, then if they are still slightly firm, to bring up to pressure once again and cook for another minute.

Trivet: Both the trivet and separators are invaluable, for they keep the vegetables above the liquid so that they retain a firm texture, see stages 3 and 5.

Liquid: You need water in the pan, see stage 2.

Pressure: Bring rapidly to H/15 lb pressure.

Reducing pressure: Under cold water.

STEP BY STEP TO PERFECT VEGETABLES

1   Prepare the vegetable(s) as usual, see points above. Do not soak green vegetables in water for a long period, as vitamin C is soluble in water. The best method of preparing green vegetables is to wash, then shred or chop just before cooking.

2   Put 280 ml (½ pt) water and the trivet into the cooker.

3   Some vegetables can be placed on the trivet, e.g. potatoes, carrots, other root vegetables. Either mix or keep them separate as desired.

4   Add a little salt, then place the open cooker over a high heat until the water just reaches boiling point.

5   Place the separators into the cooker containing other vegetables, e.g. peas, beans, finely diced root vegetables, shredded cabbage, etc. (see the times on the next pages). Add a little salt to these vegetables.

6   Fix the cover, bring to H/15 lb pressure over a high heat.

7   Lower the heat and time the cooking, then reduce the pressure immediately under cold water.

8   Remove the cover, lift out the vegetables, put into a hot serving dish and top with butter or margarine and chopped herbs.

9   Use the liquid remaining in the pan in a soup or sauce or gravy, for this liquid contains flavour and vitamins from concentrated vegetable juices.

TIMES FOR COOKING VEGETABLES

The times shown by each vegetable are based upon cooking at H/15 lb pressure. You will find the basic steps to cooking vegetables on page 111-115, together with the recommended amount of liquid and advice on seasoning. The letters T and S by the timing indicate whether a trivet or separator is used. Where there are no capital letters it means the vegetables are cooked in the liquid.

Sauces: Many vegetables can be coated with a white, cheese or parsley sauce (recipes page 53). When making the sauce use some of the liquid from the cooker instead of using all milk. The vegetable liquid contains mineral salts and adds flavour to the sauce.

Herbs: Many herbs give an interesting flavour to vegetables and these are suggested where relevant. Chop the herbs and sprinkle sparingly on the vegetables before cooking.

ARTICHOKES – GLOBE
4–10 mins T

Pull away the tough outer leaves, trim the base of the stalks and the top of the larger leaves. Wash in cold water. The varying times of cooking are due to the considerable difference in size. Serve hot with lemon flavoured melted butter, or remove the centre 'choke' while hot. Cool, then fill with an oil and vinegar dressing.

Gourmet Touch: Fill the centre of the cold artichoke with prawns in mayonnaise or pâté.

ARTICHOKES – JERUSALEM
4–5 mins T

Scrub, peel or scrape the vegetables, place in water to which 1–2 teaspoons lemon juice or white vinegar have been added (to keep the vegetable white). Serve with melted butter or coat with white sauce (page 53).

ASPARAGUS
2–4 mins T

Trim the ends of the stalks, wash well. Tie in bundles of 4–6 stalks. Stand upright if possible. Serve hot with seasoned melted butter, or cold with oil and vinegar dressing.

Gourmet Touch: Top with Hollandaise sauce (page 107).

AUBERGINES (EGGPLANTS)
3 mins

Slice or dice. Cook in the seasoned water or in tomato juice. Strain, toss in butter then top with chopped parsley. Tomato juice can be thickened in the open cooker to serve as a sauce.

BEANS – BROAD
4–5 mins T or S

If the beans are very young, trim the ends and cook whole on the trivet; when using older beans, remove the pods and cook the beans in the separator. Serve with melted butter or coat with white or parsley sauce (recipes page 53). Finely chopped summer savory, marjoram or basil will give a good flavour to broad beans.

BEANS – FRENCH AND RUNNER
4–5 mins T

String, but leave French beans whole, and slice runner beans. A little finely chopped garlic and parsley or tarragon or winter or summer savory add flavour. Cook extra beans to serve in a garlic-flavoured oil and vinegar dressing as a delicious salad.

BEETROOT
10–30 mins

Scrub raw beetroot, put into the cooker without the trivet. Allow 10 minutes in a generous ½ litre (1 pt) water for small beets, up to 30 minutes in a generous 1 litre (2 pt) water for the larger vegetables. Skin and serve hot (dice or slice if large) with melted butter and chopped parsley or a fairly thin white sauce (recipe page 53).

BROCCOLI
2–4 mins S

Trim the vegetable to give neat heads without an excessive amount of stalk or any older tough leaves. Serve with melted butter or coat in a white or cheese sauce (see page 53).

Gourmet Touch: Coat with Hollandaise sauce (see page 107), or put into a heatproof dish and top with grated cheese, fine breadcrumbs and melted butter. Brown under a hot grill for a few minutes.

CABBAGE
2–4 mins S

Prepare the cabbage just before cooking, as described on page 110. Allow the shorter time if you like slightly crisp greens. Red cabbage should be cooked apart from any other vegetables, since it tends to 'bleed' and discolour other food. Strain, toss in hot butter.

Gourmet Touch: Blend the cooked cabbage with fried chopped onions and fried chopped apples.

CARROTS
4 mins T or S

Scrub really young carrots, do not peel. Remove peel from older carrots and slice or dice – they are then better cooked in the separator. Serve with melted butter and chopped parsley or chives.

Gourmet Touch: **Carrots Vichy:** Cook the carrots in stock, not water, in the cooker (without the trivet or separator) for 2–3 minutes. Reduce pressure, remove the cover, add a good pinch sugar, a little chopped parsley and small knob of butter then cook in the open pan until the liquid evaporates.

CAULIFLOWER
2–5 mins T or S

Divide into small sprigs (flowerets) which are better cooked in the separator; or halve or quarter the vegetable and place on the trivet. Serve as broccoli.

CELERIAC
2–4 mins T or S

Peel and cut into 2.5 cm/1 inch cubes.

CELERY
2–4 mins T

Wash well, remove any hard outer sticks. Either cut into neat pieces, or quarter or halve the celery heart. Serve coated with a white or cheese sauce (as on page 53). Celery is excellent served in a tomato sauce. The recipe on page 105 is very suitable.

Gourmet Touch: Braise celery hearts as described on page 84.

CHICORY – ALSO SEAKALE AND SALSIFY
3–6 mins

These vegetables are better if cooked in the base of the cooker in butter then a little liquid. Wash chicory, do not cut; scrape seakale gently, do not cut; scrape salsify, cut into even lengths. Toss the vegetable in about 50 g (2 oz) butter, and then add 140 ml (¼ pt) water, 1 teaspoon lemon juice and seasoning. Bring to H/15 lb, lower the heat, then time as above, according to size.

COURGETTES
2–4 mins T or S

Remove hard ends, do not peel. Either halve lengthways and place on the trivet, or slice and put into the separator. Serve with melted butter and parsley or coat with white or cheese sauce, page 53.

LEEKS

4 mins T

Trim green ends and wash well in between the folds. Slit lengthways if large. Flavour with chopped parsley or rosemary.

Gourmet Touch: Braise whole leeks as described on page 84.

MARROW

4 mins T

Peel and cut older marrow into thick slices, but leave peel on younger marrow and then slice. Remove seeds where they have formed. Serve as courgettes.

ONIONS

4–8 mins T or S

If you peel and slice the onions cook in the separator; if left whole use the trivet. You could par-cook in the pressure cooker then complete cooking in the oven by roasting in a little fat.

Gourmet Touch: Braise whole onions as described on page 84.

PARSNIPS

4 mins

Peel and dice the parsnips. Cook in the liquid rather than on the trivet. You can shorten pressure cooking time to 2 minutes, strain, and then roast round a joint in the oven. Serve as carrots.

PEAS

3–4 mins S

Cook mange-tout peas whole, shell other peas. Add mint to flavour. Serve with melted butter.

Gourmet Touch: **Pois à la Française:** Put a layer of damp lettuce leaves in the separator, then the shelled peas, chopped shallots or spring onions, butter, seasoning and a final layer of damp lettuce. The lettuce can be eaten with the peas.

PEPPERS – RED AND GREEN

4–5 mins T

Cut into rings, discard core and seeds. Excellent mixed with other vegetables.

POTATOES
4–5 mins T

Scrape new, peel old, or leave the skin on the potatoes. Dice large potatoes evenly. Toss in melted butter and chopped parsley.

Jacket Potatoes: Scrub, but do not peel large potatoes. Cook for 12 minutes on the trivet, using generous ½ litre (1 pt) water. Remove from the cooker, cut a slice from the potatoes and top with butter.

PUMPKIN AND SQUASH
4-12 mins T or S

Cut in half if small, or peel and slice or cut into dice or leave whole if pattypan.

SPINACH
0 mins

Wash, but do not drain spinach. Put into the open cooker, heat gently until the juice flows, press down hard, add more spinach with a little seasoning. Do not have the cooker more than two-thirds full. Fix the cover, bring to pressure, then reduce pressure immediately. Strain, then blend with butter or chop and blend with a little thick cream and butter.

SPRING GREENS AND SPROUTS
(Brussels) 2–4 mins S

As cabbage.

SWEDES AND TURNIPS
4 mins

As parsnips.

SWEETCORN (CORN ON THE COB)
3–5 mins T

Remove the husk (leaves round the cob), place on trivet, season very lightly. Serve with melted butter.

TOMATOES
0 mins T or S

Place firm tomatoes on the trivet or in the separator, season lightly. Fix cover, bring to pressure then reduce pressure immediately. Chopped basil or tarragon blend well with tomatoes.

FROZEN VEGETABLES

As frozen vegetables are partially cooked (in the process of blanching) before freezing, it is essential they are not overcooked.

If, therefore, you allow the same cooking time as for fresh vegetables it will compensate for the thawing period. You may not, however, find it worthwhile to cook frozen vegetables in the cooker unless part of a meal. Use the separator and do not defrost before cooking.

DRIED BEANS AND PULSES

Beans and pulses provide important and economical protein in family meals.

These traditional type of dried vegetables are best with a minimum of 12 hours soaking in cold water (or stock gives extra flavour) to cover, or put them into a large basin (allow room for expansion since dried beans will more than double in volume when soaked). Add enough boiling water to cover the vegetables. Place a plate on top, leave for an hour.

Beans and pulses can be cooked in a pressure cooker without soaking first but soaking reduces the cooking time and there is the advantage of being able to dispose of the soaking water which can help reduce the gaseous affects of eating beans. Lentils do not require soaking but some people prefer to give them a short soak.

For unsoaked beans and pulses allow about twice the cooking times for soaked ones.

Exact cooking times are very difficult for dried vegetables since their cooking times will vary widely depending on how old the beans are and their degree of dryness. But they are forgiving foods and a few minutes over is unlikely to cause disaster.

Do not add salt to the beans or pulses until they are cooked as salt hardens their skins and prevents them softening.

A tablespoon of oil added to the cooking water will help stop the water foaming while the beans are cooking.

Whichever method you choose, they are then ready to cook.

1   Strain the liquid in which the vegetables were soaked, add enough extra fresh liquid to give the required amount, as stage 2.

2   Place the liquid into the cooker. Allow at least 1 litre (2 pt) liquid to each 225 g (8 oz) dried vegetables. Remember that the cooked vegetables expand to nearly three times the original weight.

3   Bring the liquid to the boil, add the soaked vegetables, bring once

more to the boil, remove any scum from the top of the liquid. Add a tablespoon of oil.

4 Do not fill the pressure cooker to more than half full, including the liquid.

5 Fix the lid in place, bring gradually to H/15 lb. Lower the heat and time the cooking period:

Adzuki beans	6-8 mins
Black beans	8-12 mins
Borlotti beans	12 mins
Butter beans	30 mins
Cannellini beans	12 mins
Chick peas	24 mins
Flageolet beans	6-8 mins
Haricot beans (small)	20 mins
(large)	30 mins
Lentils	10 mins
Peas (marrowfat)	
(split)	15 mins
(whole)	20 mins
Red kidney beans	9-12 mins
Soya beans	30 mins

5 Allow the pressure to drop at room temperature, and then serve the beans, peas or lentils.

6 Clean the lid and vents thoroughly after cooking beans and pulses as the foam that forms when they cook can clog up the mechanisms.

They can be tossed in butter and chopped herbs, coated with a sauce, or added to stews and salads.

BOSTON BAKED BEANS

Serves 8
Pressure cooking time 20 mins

250 g/ 8 oz haricot beans
400 g tin chopped tomatoes
50 g /2 oz caster sugar

1 onion, finely chopped
2 teaspoons mustard powder
1 tablespoon treacle
Salt and pepper

---

1   Place the beans in a bowl and cover with boiling water.

2   Leave for 1 hour and discard the water.

3   Place the beans and remaining ingredients in the pressure cooker with 425 ml/¾ pt water.

4   Bring to H/15 lb and cook for 20 minutes.

5   Release pressure slowly.

6   If there is too much liquid left in the pan reduce by boiling down.

DHAL

Serves 4
Pressure cooking time 5 mins

---

2 tablespoons oil
1 onion, chopped
2.5 cm/1" piece fresh ginger, peeled and sliced
1 teaspoon cumin seeds
1 teaspoon ground coriander
½ teaspoon turmeric
250 g/8 oz split red lentils

---

1   Heat the oil in the pan and cook the onion until golden.

2   Add the ginger, cumin, coriander and turmeric and cook for 1 minute stirring.

3   Add the lentils and 300 ml/½ pt water.

4   Bring to the boil and skim the surface of any foam.

5   Place on cover and bring to H/15 lb.

6   Cook for 5 minutes.

7   Release pressure slowly.

COOKING RICE, PASTA AND CEREALS

Both rice and pasta (spaghetti, macaroni, etc.) form the basis of many interesting meals. These foods are also excellent accompaniments to meat, fish and poultry dishes. It is simple and relatively quick to cook coarse oatmeal in the pressure cooker to make traditional porridge, and barley to add to savoury dishes.

POINTS TO REMEMBER

Quantities to allow: These foods expand during cooking. Since they absorb liquid, they increase in weight, e.g. 25 g (1 oz) rice (a small portion for one person) becomes nearly 75 g (3 oz) when cooked, so do not be too generous with amounts.

*Timing: This is important as you spoil the texture of the foods if overcooked; times are given under the different foods.

Trivet: Do not use this, for the foods are cooked *in* the liquid; you can have the trivet in the cooker when rice is cooked in a solid container, as described on page 120.

Liquid As all these foods absorb liquid, use the full quantities given in the recipes. You use less liquid than when cooking in a saucepan, since it does not evaporate. Bring the liquid to the boil in the open cooker, add the rice, pasta or cereal, stir briskly, and then fix the cover.

Seasoning: Add salt or other seasoning to taste; since a smaller quantity of liquid is used be a little sparing with seasoning, adding more later if desired.

Filling the cooker: All these foods tend to rise in cooking, so the base of the pan should be no more than one-third filled with food and liquid.

Pressure: Bring rapidly to H/15 lb pressure, lower the heat rather more than usual, although pressure must be maintained. This is to make sure none of the starchy liquid rises to block the vent.

Reducing pressure: When cooking rice or pasta, reduce the pressure with cold water, but when cooking oatmeal or barley allow pressure to drop at room temperature.

Note: This applies to the traditional types of foods. Very quick-cooking varieties are cooked almost as quickly in a saucepan.

If you prefer to cook them in a pressure cooker, allow about one-third of the recommended time on the packet, at H/15 lb pressure.

TO BOIL RICE

Serves 3–4 (depending on meal)
Pressure cooking time 5 mins

1 Choose long grain rice for savoury dishes; it is less starchy. To each 100 g (4 oz) allow 280 ml (½ pt) water. If you prefer more home-ly measures then use an average teacup, if filled nearly to the brim it equals 100 g (4 oz), and 2 teacups water.

2 Pour the water into the cooker, add ½ level teaspoon salt (or a lit-tle less if preferred); bring the water to the boil, add the rice. Many kinds of rice are pre-washed, but if you wash the rice in cold water do so immediately before cooking.

3 Stir briskly, fix the cover and bring to H/15 lb pressure. Lower the heat and cook for 5 minutes.

4 Reduce pressure under cold water.

5 If you are in a hurry, strain and rinse the rice through a sieve, to separate the grains, shake dry. If you have time rinse as above, spread on to a hot dish; put into a pre-heated oven. Turn off the oven heat and leave the rice to dry in the residual heat.

TO VARY:

When other foods are in the pressure cooker place the rice, water and salt into a solid container (ovenproof dish), cover with buttered paper, cook as above, but reduce pressure at room temperature.

FREEZING RICE, PASTA AND CEREALS

Since these foods cook quickly, freezing is hardly necessary. Cereals and pasta tend to lose texture in freezing, but rice freezes well. Cool the cooked rice, pack in the container; lightly freeze, then separate the grains and continue freezing.

To reheat; drop into boiling liquid, bring just to the boil again.

FLAVOURINGS FOR RICE

Curried Rice: Fry 1 chopped onion in 25 g (1 oz) fat in the open cooker, add 1–2 teaspoons curry powder, cook for 1 minute, then proceed as stages 1–5 on page 120. For a more interesting curried rice do not rinse the rice, add a few sultanas, a little desiccated coconut, diced cooked vegetables, diced cooked meat, fish or poultry, and heat gently in the open cooker until the right consistency is obtained.

Lemon Rice: A slice of lemon (free from pips) helps to whiten boiled rice, but if you add finely grated lemon rind and about 1 tablespoon lemon juice it gives a pleasant flavour to rice to serve with fish or poultry. Put the lemon with the water at stage 2, left.

Saffron Rice: This gives a pleasant yellow colour and flavour to rice and is particularly good with curry. Add either a good pinch of saffron powder or a few saffron strands to the water at stage 2, left. You can infuse the strands in cold water, then strain if you do not want these in the dish.

Savoury Rice: Cook the rice in stock or tomato juice instead of water or add finely chopped onion, tomatoes, green and red peppers at stage 2, left.

Sweet Rice: Milk puddings, using rice, are described on pages 136-137, but if you want a pleasant change, cook long grain rice in fruit juice or a thin fruit purée instead of in water. Add sugar to taste instead of salt, follow stages 1–4, pages 120.

RICE AS AN ACCOMPANIMENT

Rice is an excellent accompaniment to many dishes and there are various ways of cooking it with other foods in the pressure cooker.

If you have fish or other solid foods on the trivet, then cook the rice in a container, as described. When cooked, rinse and drain or dry out in the oven and serve.

If you are cooking moist food, such as a curry or stew then there are two ways to deal with the meal:

a) Cook the rice in the pan, and dry out (and also keep warm) in the oven while cooking the rest of the meal.

b) Cook the stew, spoon into the serving dish, keep hot while the rice is cooked in the pressure cooker.

RISOTTO

The Italian word denotes a rice mixture and this can be varied in many ways. Use the Italian arborio or carnaroli rice, which gives a transparent look when cooked; failing that use long grain rice for a drier, or round grain for a stickier texture, according to personal choice. These dishes serve 4.

Risotto alla Milanese: Chop a medium onion, fry in 25 g (1 oz) butter and 1 tablespoon oil in the open cooker. Add a generous ½ litre (1 pt) saffron-flavoured stock, bring to the boil, add 225 g (8 oz) rice and cook as stages 1–4 on page 120. Dry out slightly in the open cooker and serve topped with grated parmesan cheese.

Risotto alla Finanziera: As above, but add 50 g (2 oz) sliced mushrooms and 6–8 chicken livers to the onion. Omit the saffron.

Chicken Fricassée: The classic dish is made by adding diced cooked chicken to a white sauce (made as on page 53 with chicken stock and milk), but you can make a delicious variation by adding about 225 g (8 oz) diced uncooked chicken to the onion in the first risotto recipe.

TO BOIL PASTA

Serves 4
Pressure cooking time see stage 3

1   Allow approximately 225 g (8 oz) pasta for 4 people. Macaroni, spaghetti, similar pasta shapes, and larger noodles need a generous 1 litre (2 pt) water for this quantity. The very tiny alphabet noodles can be cooked with ¾ litre (1½ pt).

2   Pour the water into the cooker, add 1 level teaspoon salt; bring the water to the boil, lower the pasta into the liquid. The long spaghetti should be broken into shorter lengths.

3   Stir briskly, fix the cover and bring to H/15 lb pressure. Lower the heat and time as follows; regular spaghetti and elbow macaroni take 5–6 minutes; finer spaghetti and short lengths of macaroni 4–5 minutes; and very fine vermicelli or similar shapes and alphabet noodles 3–4 minutes. It is better to cook for the shorter period, check the pasta – it should be 'al dente', i.e. cooked, but still firm to the touch, when pressed with a fork. Reduce the pressure.

4   Strain the pasta, return to the cooker with a generous knob of butter and a little chopped parsley. Mix and serve as an accompaniment, or use as suggested in the dishes on this page.

TO SERVE PASTA AS AN ACCOMPANIMENT

To cook pasta to serve together with other food, it is advisable either to:

   a) Cook the pasta, as above. Strain well, toss in butter, put into a hot dish and cover tightly. Keep warm while cooking the rest of the food.

   b) Cook the sauce or stew; spoon into a hot dish, keep hot while cooking the pasta.

DISHES USING PASTA

Macaroni Cheese: In this dish only 75 g (3 oz) macaroni is required. Cook this, as described, in just under ½ litre (1 pt) salted water (stages 2 and 3). Meanwhile make a cheese sauce as on page 53, but use 40 g (1½ oz) butter, 40 g (1½ oz) flour, 420 ml (¾ pt) milk, seasoning and 100 g (4 oz) grated cheese. Blend the drained macaroni with the sauce, put into a hot, heatproof dish, top with more grated cheese, fine crumbs and a little melted butter or margarine and brown under the grill for a few minutes. Serves 4.

Spaghetti alla Bolognese: Make the Bolognese sauce, as on page 104, keep hot, and then cook the spaghetti. Drain the spaghetti, put on to a hot dish, top with the sauce and serve with grated parmesan cheese.

Spaghetti alla Milanese: Use Tomato sauce, on page 105, instead of the meat sauce, above.

PORRIDGE

Serves 3–4
Pressure cooking time 15–20 mins

1   Allow about 4 teacups water to each teacup coarse oatmeal. If you prefer to weigh the food then it is about 100 g (4 oz) oatmeal to a generous ½ litre (1 pt) water.

2   Pour the water into the cooker, add a generous pinch salt (more if desired); bring the water to the boil. Add the oatmeal, stir briskly.

3   Fix the cover, bring to H/15 lb pressure. Lower the heat then time the cooking:

Allow only 15 minutes if you like a thick porridge; allow pressure to drop at room temperature, remove the cover and stir over a low heat until thickened.

Allow 20 minutes for a thinner porridge with a smoother texture.

4   Serve with extra salt or sugar and hot or cold milk.

TO VARY:

Barley and Pearl Barley: This is cooked in the same way as oatmeal above. Allow 20 minutes at H/15 lb pressure.

PUDDINGS AND CAKES

To many people it is a surprise to learn that steamed puddings – ranging from a light sponge to a rich Christmas pudding – and egg custards are among the desserts that can be cooked under pressure.

It is well worthwhile using this method of cooking, since you save time, which means you save fuel, and you avoid steam in the kitchen. And there is no need to check on water, or oven temperature in the case of an egg custard.

Naturally there is a correct technique in steaming puddings or making egg custards in a pressure cooker, just as there is by any other method, and this is outlined on this page and pages 125-127 and 134.

You will find it simple to cook fruit and fruit sauces successfully in the pressure cooker.

TO STEAM A PUDDING OR CAKE

Naturally the cooking time in a pressure cooker will vary according to the weight and the richness of the mixture. You will find the pressure cooking time at the head of most recipes, except in the case of a Christmas pudding, where it is outlined in some detail on pages 129-130, stage 4. In addition there is a steaming time given as well. The reason for this is explained on page 125-126.

TO PREPARE A PUDDING OR CAKE

The mixture: Make the recipe exactly as usual, taking the same care to blend the ingredients carefully. You may find the hints under sponge puddings, page 130, and suet puddings, page 127, helpful.

Choosing the cooking utensil: While it is usual to steam puddings in a china or ovenproof glass basin, you can use a soufflé dish or a metal or special polythene basin (check it is guaranteed for boiling and is not the type sold only for storing food), or a seamless cake tin which you would generally choose for a cake.

For the quickest results choose metal or polythene. Always make quite sure the utensil is sufficiently large; the uncooked pudding or cake mixture should only two-thirds fill the basin or other container, thus allowing plenty of space for the pudding or cake to rise during cooking.

If you would rather use china or ovenproof glass, then increase the pressure cooking time by 5 minutes for small puddings or 10 minutes for larger puddings or cakes.

Preparing for cooking: Grease the basin, dish or tin well. Put in the mixture and cover with a double thickness of greaseproof paper or foil. Greaseproof paper allows the steam to penetrate through to the mixture whereas foil, which is not porous, does not. That does not matter, except that you should allow an extra 5–10 minutes cooking time when using foil.

Grease the greaseproof paper or foil, make a pleat in the middle to give extra space for the pudding or cake to rise. Place over the pudding or cake, the greased side next to the mixture. Either tie firmly in position or tuck the edges in so securely that the paper or foil cannot move during cooking.

In order to remove the hot pudding from the pressure cooker, make a string handle, as shown in figs. 1 and 2, or take a long piece of foil, fold this into a strip – of two to three thicknesses – and put under the pudding. Make sure you have long ends you can hold, see fig. 3, these can be folded over the pudding while cooking.

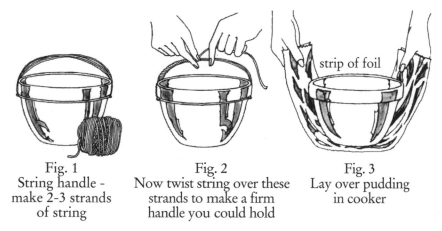

Fig. 1
String handle –
make 2-3 strands
of string

Fig. 2
Now twist string over these
strands to make a firm
handle you could hold

Fig. 3
Lay over pudding
in cooker

Trivet: Always use the trivet in the pressure cooker when cooking steamed puddings and cakes; this keeps the mixture above the level of the water.

Liquid: Pour at least 850 ml (1½ pt) boiling water into the pan; do not let this continue boiling, and evaporating, before placing the pudding or cake on the trivet in the pressure pan and fixing the cover. It is a good idea to add a tablespoon lemon juice or vinegar to the water to prevent the pan from discolouring.

Timing: The timing for steamed puddings and cakes is in two stages:
a) Steaming: As pudding and cake mixtures generally contain a raising agent which makes the mixture rise, it is advisable to steam for the first part of the cooking period. This enables the raising agent to react satisfactorily. If you do not give this initial steaming, the

pudding or cake could be heavy and close-textured. It is also better to steam a Christmas pudding for a time to give a better texture. Do not, therefore, put the pressure weight on the cooker, or lower the control lever until the end of the steaming period. Steaming should be over a low heat, just as though you were using an ordinary saucepan, only a gentle flow of steam should come from the cooker. If the heat is too high and the steam too vigorous, the liquid could evaporate during the steaming period and leave the pan dry.

b) Pressure cooking: At the end of the steaming period, simply put on the weight or lower the control lever and bring to L/5 lb (or H/15 lb where indicated) and follow the pressure cooking time given in the recipe.

If you wish to pressure-cook one of your own favourite steamed puddings, and the recipe is not in this book; choose a similar type of pudding, use approximately the same amount of mixture and follow the directions accordingly.

As a guide here are the times to follow:

NORMAL COOKING TIME	IN A PRESSURE COOKER	
	STEAMING	AT L/5 LB
30 minutes	5 minutes	10 minutes
1 hour	15 minutes	25 minutes
2 hours	20 minutes	50 minutes
3 hours	20 minutes	60 minutes

Pressure: Steamed puddings are better cooked at L/5 lb pressure (with the exception of the Christmas pudding or similar recipes).

Most cookers have variable pressures, i.e. L/5 lb; M/10 lb; and H/15 lb. If your particular model has only H/15 lb pressure and you enjoy making and eating steamed puddings, it may be worth your while to buy a model on which you can alter the pressure.

You *can* cook all puddings at H/15 lb pressure, but the results, particularly in the case of sponge puddings, may not be quite as good as when cooked at L/5 lb pressure.

If you make several smaller-sized puddings instead of one larger one the results will be better on H/15 lb. Naturally, if you have to cook puddings at H/15 lb pressure you will allow the same steaming period but deduct 5 minutes if the pressure cooking time is under 30 minutes, i.e. a recipe that takes 25 minutes at L/5 lb pressure will need only 20 minutes at L/5 lb pressure.

Deduct 10 minutes if the pressure cooking time is over 30 minutes, so that a pudding which takes 40 minutes at L/5 lb pressure needs only 30 minutes at H/15 lb pressure.

Reducing pressure: Allow the pressure to drop at room temperature so that the pudding or cake remains light. You will find that if you time the cooking period so that you remove the pressure cooker from the heat just before dishing up the first course of a meal, the pressure will have dropped and you can remove the cover. The pudding can then be served at just the right time and will be piping hot.

COOKING TIMES IN RECIPES

As stated under *Choosing the cooking utensil,* on page 124, it is quicker to cook the pudding if you use a metal or polythene basin and cover it with greased greaseproof paper. Additional time must be added if using china or ovenproof glass and foil.

The pressure cooking times that follow are based upon the use of metal and greaseproof paper. If you want to depart from this, just check pages 124-125.

SUET PUDDINGS

One of the most adaptable puddings is made by preparing a suet crust pastry, as given in the Steak and Kidney pudding, page 98, and filling it with sweetened fruit.

FRUIT PUDDINGS

Suet crust pastry made with 170–225 g (6–8 oz) flour, etc., as recipe on page 98
450 g (1 lb) fruit (weight when prepared)
Sugar to taste
Little water

---

1   Prepare the pastry and line the basin as in stages 1 and 2, page 99.

2   Put in the prepared fruit and sugar to taste. Use several tablespoons water with firm fruits, but little, if any, water with soft fruits.

3   Cover the pudding as described in stages 4–6 on page 99 and cook as the Steak and Kidney pudding, but allow the following times:

steaming time 15 mins
pressure cooking time 25 mins

4   Allow the pressure to drop at room temperature, then serve the hot pudding with cream or custard.

SEASONAL SUGGESTIONS:

Spring: Use rhubarb and gooseberries.

Summer: Use the many berry fruits.

Autumn: Use blackberries, plums, damsons (if hard, pre-cook a little).

Winter: Apples and pre-cooked dried fruits (see page 144).

ECONOMICAL CHRISTMAS PUDDING

This is a particularly light pudding which would be enjoyed by people who find the traditional pudding a little rich.

Serves 6–8
Steaming time see stage 4, pages 129-130
Pressure cooking time see stage 4, pages 129-130

---

125 g (5 oz) apple (weight when peeled)
125 g (5 oz) carrots (weight when peeled)
225 g (8 oz) seedless raisins
50 g (2 oz) sultanas
50 g (2 oz) currants
225 g (8 oz) soft breadcrumbs
50 g (2 oz) self-raising flour (or plain flour and ½ teaspoon baking powder)
½ teaspoon mixed spice
½ teaspoon ground nutmeg
100 g (4 oz) melted butter or margarine
125 g (5 oz) moist brown sugar
1 tablespoon orange marmalade
1 tablespoon golden syrup or black treacle
4 tablespoons milk or ale
1 egg

---

1 Peel and grate the apples and carrots.

2 Mix with all the other ingredients.

3 Divide into the required size basins. Although the ingredients in this recipe are not the same as in the more traditional pudding on the right, the total weight of mixture is very similar, so you can divide into the same sized containers and cook for the same time.

This pudding should not be made more than a few days before Christmas Day. Reheat in exactly the same way as described under stage 7, page 130.

Gourmet Touch: **Brandy Butter:** Cream 170 g (6 oz) butter with approximately 250 g (9 oz) sieved icing sugar, then gradually beat in 3–4 tablespoons brandy. Chill well; serve with the pudding.

CHRISTMAS PUDDING

This traditional rich pudding is improved if you make it some weeks before Christmas, and allow it time to mature with storage.

The metric measures are given more exactly in this recipe, so the total bulk of mixture is almost identical to that made with imperial measures. Prepare dried fruit carefully. If washing this, dry at room temperature for 48 hours.

Serves 6–8
Steaming time see stage 4
Pressure cooking time see stage 4

---

1 lemon
1 medium carrot
1 small dessert apple
110 g (4 oz) candied peel
55–110 g (2–4 oz) blanched almonds
55 g (2 oz) plain or self-raising flour
1 teaspoon mixed spice
½–1 teaspoon ground cinnamon
110 g (4 oz) soft breadcrumbs
110 g (4 oz) moist brown sugar
110 g (4 oz) shredded suet or melted butter
1 tablespoon black treacle
450 g (1 lb) mixed dried fruit – use rather more raisins than currants and sultanas
2 large eggs
4–8 tablespoons* ale, beer, stout, brandy or whisky

*Use smaller quantity if you like a firm pudding that slices neatly, and the larger quantity for a moist crumbly texture.

---

1   Grate the zest (top part of the rind) from the lemon, squeeze out the juice.

2   Peel and chop the carrot and apple and chop the peel and almonds.

3   Mix all the ingredients together, stir well and wish hard – get all the family to stir for good luck. I like to leave the pudding overnight before cooking; I find it gives the flavours a chance to blend better.

4   The mixture will produce a total weight of nearly 1½ kg (3 lb), so you can divide and cook the mixture in various ways. You could make 6–8 individual puddings, or three small, or two medium, or

one large and one small; cook as follows:

	Steaming	Pressure Cooking– H/15 lb
individual	10 mins	50 mins
small – ½ kg (1 lb)	15 mins	1¼ hours
medium – ¾ kg (1½ lb)	20 mins	2¼ hours
large – 1 kg (2 lb)	20 mins	3 hours

The pressure cooking time could be exceeded slightly without harming the pudding. See pages 125-126 for the amount of water needed and full instructions on cooking steamed puddings.

5 Cover the pudding basins, stand on the trivet, add boiling water, bring up to pressure steadily and time the cooking as above.

6 Allow the pressure to drop, and then remove the puddings. Take off the damp covers, allow puddings to cool, put on dry covers and store in a cool place.

7 On Christmas Day, or when required, heat at H/15 lb pressure as follows:

> Individual puddings: 10 mins
> ½ kg (1 lb) puddings: 20 mins
> ¾ kg (1½lb) puddings: 30 mins
> 1 kg (2 lb) puddings: 30 mins

TO VARY:

Golden Christmas Pudding: This makes a paler coloured pudding which is a pleasant change from the darker one. Cook as the recipe above. Omit the spice, cinnamon, and use 450 g (1 lb) golden sultanas instead of the mixed fruit.

Add 100 g (4 oz) chopped, dried, uncooked apricots. Use golden syrup in place of black treacle and mix with a pale sweet sherry.

Gourmet Touch: Spoon *warmed* brandy or rum over the pudding and ignite before serving. Serve with brandy butter, see page 128.

SPONGE PUDDINGS

You can achieve a really featherlight sponge with careful blending of the ingredients and correct cooking in the pressure cooker.

In order to obtain a smooth, light texture:

Cream the margarine, or butter, and sugar until really soft and light;

do not melt the fat – this prevents air being incorporated into the mixture, see one-stage mixture also, on page 132. Beat the eggs in gradually; add a little sieved flour, if the mixture shows signs of curdling.

Do not over-beat the mixture when adding the sieved flour.

Steam for the recommended period before bringing to pressure; for details of this method see page 130.

PLAIN SPONGE PUDDING

Serves 4
Steaming time 15 mins
Pressure cooking time 25 mins

---

110 g (4 oz) margarine or butter
110 g (4 oz) caster sugar
2 large eggs
110 g (4 oz) self-raising flour (or plain flour and 1 teaspoon baking powder)

---

1   Cream the margarine, or butter, and sugar until soft and light in texture.

2   Gradually beat in the eggs.

3   Sieve the flour or flour and baking powder; fold this gently and carefully into the creamed mixture.

4   Grease and flour a 1-litre (1¾-pt) basin, or even a slightly larger one, spoon in the mixture.

5   Cover the basin, see page 125.

6   Stand the pudding on the trivet in the cooker; add a generous ¾ litre (1½ pt) boiling water.

7   Steam for 15 minutes, and then bring steadily to L/5 lb pressure.

8   Cook for 25 minutes; allow the pressure to drop.

9   Turn the pudding out of the basin on to a hot serving dish and serve with hot jam or one of the sauces on page 133.

FLAVOURINGS FOR SPONGE PUDDINGS

All puddings are cooked as recipe above.

Blackcap Pudding: Put 2–3 tablespoons of a dark jelly or jam, e.g. bramble jelly, damson or blackcurrant jam, at the bottom of the basin then add the sponge mixture. Any jam or jelly can be used, giving a name to the pudding, e.g. greengage jam would give Greencap Pudding.

Chocolate Pudding: Omit 1 tablespoon flour, sieve 1 tablespoon cocoa powder with the flour. Serve with Chocolate or Coffee sauce, see page 133.

Chocolate Chip Pudding: Make either the plain sponge on page 131, or the chocolate variation above; add 50 g (2 oz) chocolate chips or chopped plain chocolate to the mixture. This remains firm in cooking.

Coffee Pudding: Use small eggs; mix 1–2 teaspoons instant coffee powder with 1 tablespoon hot water, blend with the eggs. Serve with Coffee or Chocolate sauce, page 133.

Fruit Puddings: Add 75–100 g (3–4 oz) dried fruit to the sponge mixture or put a layer of *well-drained* canned, cooked or mashed soft fruit at the bottom of the basin, then add the sponge mixture.

Ginger Pudding: Sieve 1–2 teaspoons ground ginger with the flour, add syrup as in the Golden Pudding, below.

Golden Pudding: Put 2–3 tablespoons golden syrup at the bottom of the basin then add the sponge mixture.

ADAPTATIONS OF PLAIN SPONGE PUDDING

Economical Pudding: Use only 50 g (2 oz) margarine or butter, 50 g (2 oz) caster sugar, 1 egg, 110 g (4 oz) flour and milk to make a soft dropping consistency.

One-Stage Mixture: If using one of the soft 'luxury' margarines, put all the ingredients for the sponge pudding into a basin and stir for 2 minutes only.

CANNED PUDDINGS

Read the instructions on the can for reheating these puddings.

If you leave the pudding in the can, check to see if the can needs to be opened. Allow one-third of the recommended cooking time on the can at H/15 lb pressure.

You can transfer the cooked pudding from the can to a greased basin. Cover with greased greaseproof paper and cook for 5 minutes at H/15 lb pressure.

BASED UPON A SPONGE PUDDING

The following recipe is based upon the plain or flavoured sponge mixtures on pages 130-131 with slight adaptations.

CASTLE PUDDINGS

These individual puddings are most attractive in appearance and can be made according to the basic plain sponge or any of the flavourings given on pages 130-132.

If you are using a pressure cooker that does not give L/5 lb pressure, you get a better sponge pudding at H/15 lb pressure if you use individual containers rather than one larger basin.

1   Make the selected sponge mixture, see pages 130-132.

2   Grease four small basins or cups.

3   Put in the mixture; do not fill the containers more than two-thirds full. Cover well, see page 125.

4   Stand on the trivet and add a generous ¾ litre (1½ pt) boiling water.

5   Steam for 5 minutes, and then bring steadily to either L/5 lb pressure or H/15 lb pressure, according to the particular cooker.

6   Cook for 5 minutes at pressure, unless you have a layer of fruit, then allow 8 minutes; allow the pressure to drop.

7   Turn out the puddings and serve.

SAUCES FOR PUDDINGS

Chocolate Sauce 1: Blend 1 tablespoon cornflour, 1 tablespoon cocoa powder, 2 tablespoons sugar and 280 ml (½ pt) milk together. Pour into a pan, add 25 g (1 oz) butter, stir over a low heat until thickened.

Chocolate Sauce 2: Melt 175 g (6 oz) plain chocolate, 25 g (1 oz) butter and 140 ml (¼ pt) milk or water, in a basin over a pan of hot water.

Coffee Sauce: Blend 1 tablespoon cornflour and 2 tablespoons sugar with 140 ml (¼ pt) strong coffee and 140 ml (¼ pt) milk. Pour into pan, add 25 g (1 oz) butter, stir over a low heat to thicken.

Lemon Sauce: Blend the finely grated zest (yellow part of the rind), of 1 lemon, 2 tablespoons lemon juice, 50 g (2 oz) sugar, 2 teaspoons arrowroot or cornflour and 280 ml (½ pt) water, then stir over a low heat until thickened and clear.

FREEZING PUDDINGS AND CAKES

Suet and sponge puddings and cakes can be prepared, put into the cooking utensil, and then frozen. Defrost and cook as the recipe.

If you cook the cake or pudding before freezing, defrost at room temperature. Reheat puddings for 5 minutes at H/15 lb pressure. A cooked egg custard does not freeze well; you can, however, freeze the uncooked mixture. Defrost this and cook as the recipe.

EGG CUSTARDS

When one thinks of the care that usually has to be taken to cook an egg custard either by steaming over hot, but not boiling, water or in a bain-marie in a slow oven, it may seem improbable to cook the mixture in the heat of a pressure cooker. The fact remains that egg custard, and the many dishes based upon this mixture of eggs and liquid, are highly successful in the pressure cooker. If you want a lightly set and less rich custard use the smaller quantity of eggs or egg yolks. A high proportion of egg yolks, as opposed to whole eggs, gives the richest custard.

Use china, ovenproof glassware or the type of polythene used for boiling. The custards look attractive if cooked in a soufflé dish. Select one in which the custard comes more than three-quarters of the way up the dish. Grease the container lightly. Take care to cover the custard and dish thoroughly with a double thickness of well-greased greaseproof paper. This prevents the steam from making the top of the custard moist as the pressure drops at room temperature.

Serves 3–4
Pressure cooking time 5 mins

2–3 eggs or 3–4 egg yolks or 2 eggs and 1–2 egg yolks
Few drops vanilla essence
1–2 tablespoons sugar (or use vanilla-flavoured sugar and omit essence)
420 ml (¾ pt) milk
Grated nutmeg (optional)

---

1   Beat the eggs or egg yolks with the essence; do not over-beat.

2   Warm the sugar, or vanilla sugar, with the milk, then stir as you blend with the eggs.

3   Pour the mixture into the greased container; add a little nutmeg and cover well.

4   Pour 280 ml (½ pt) water into the cooker, add the trivet, then place the container on the trivet.

5   Fix the cover and bring steadily to H/15 lb pressure, lower the heat and cook for 5 minutes.

6   Allow the pressure to drop at room temperature then remove the paper.

7   Serve hot or cold.

Bread and Butter Pudding: Cut 2 or 3 thin slices of bread and butter, divide into triangles. Put into the dish with 2–3 tablespoons dried fruit. Add the egg custard and cook as recipe but allow 10 minutes at H/15 lb pressure.

FLAVOURINGS FOR EGG CUSTARD

Omit the nutmeg and vanilla from the basic recipe.

Almond Custard: Use almond essence instead of vanilla. Top with blanched almonds or with sugar and almonds and grill as in Crème Brûlée, page 136.

Coffee Custard: Dissolve 2–3 level teaspoons instant coffee in the milk or use half strong coffee and half single cream.

Chocolate Custard: Blend 1–1½ tablespoons cocoa powder with the milk, or use 2–3 tablespoons chocolate powder, or 50 g (2 oz) plain chocolate.

Chocolate Crème: Use all single cream instead of milk, or half milk and half cream, and flavour as the chocolate custard. Allow to cool and top with whipped cream and grated chocolate.

Coffee Walnut Cream: Use all single cream instead of milk, or half milk and half cream, and flavour as the coffee custard. Add 1–2 tablespoons finely chopped walnuts to the egg custard before cooking.

Lemon or Orange Custard: Flavour the custard with ½ –1 teaspoon finely grated lemon or orange zest (coloured top part of the rind). To make a more luxurious dessert allow the custard to cool, then top with a layer of lemon curd or orange marmalade and top with whipped cream. Decorate with mandarin orange segments. A mixture of single cream and milk could be used instead of all milk.

Macaroon Apricot Custard: Put 75–100 g (3–4 oz) well-drained cooked or canned apricots at the bottom of the dish. Add custard. Cook as recipe. Top with macaroon crumbs and apricots.

VIENNOISE PUDDING

Serves 4–5
Pressure cooking time 10 mins

FOR THE CARAMEL:
75 g (3 oz) sugar
3 tablespoons water

FOR THE PUDDING:
420 ml (¾ pt) milk
75 g (3 oz) bread (weight without crusts)
25–50 g (1–2 oz) glacé cherries
25 g (1 oz) candied peel

25 g (1 oz) blanched almonds
25–50 g (1–2 oz) sultanas
3 eggs or use 2 yolks and 1 whole egg
1 tablespoon sugar (optional)

---

1   Put the sugar and water into a strong pan; stir over a low heat until the sugar has dissolved. *Stop stirring* and boil steadily until golden brown.

2   Add the milk and stir over a low heat until blended.

3   Dice the bread; chop the cherries, peel and nuts and put into a basin, add the sultanas.

4   Pour the caramel liquid over this and leave for 15–30 minutes to soften the bread.

5   Add the well-beaten eggs; taste the mixture and add extra sugar if desired.

6   Pour into a soufflé dish, cover and cook as egg custard, page 134, allowing 10 minutes at H/15 lb pressure.

7   Serve hot or cold with cream.

TO VARY:

Almond Pudding: Omit the caramel and bread. Dice 2–3 macaroon biscuits and proceed as in stages 3–7. A few drops of almond essence can be added at stage 2 and another 25 g (1 oz) chopped blanched almonds.

Chocolate Crumb Pudding: Omit the caramel. Blend 1 tablespoon cocoa powder with the warm milk then proceed as in stages 3–7.

Crème Brûlée: Omit bread, cherries, peel, sultanas. Follow stages 1 and 2 above, and then blend in the eggs and sugar at stage 2. Cook as above, but allow only 5 minutes at H/15 lb pressure. Cool, then top with blanched almonds and brown sugar. Crisp under the grill.

MILK PUDDINGS

Generally a milk pudding is baked for a long period in a slow oven. It is very successful if cooked for a short time in a pressure cooker. It can then be browned under the grill if desired.

RICE PUDDING

Serves 3–4
Pressure cooking time 12 mins

15–25 g (½–1 oz) butter or pure suet
Generous ½ litre (1 pt) milk or milk plus a little single cream
2 tablespoons sugar
50 g (2 oz) pudding (round grain) rice
Flavouring – see stage 3

1   Remove the trivet and put the butter or suet into the base of the pressure cooker.

2   Melt the knob of butter or suet in the open cooker, add the milk then bring to the boil quickly.

3   Stir in the sugar, rice and any flavouring – this can be vanilla, or other essence, a strip of lemon rind (not the juice), a bay leaf, spice or cinnamon to taste, a little chocolate or cocoa powder, coffee essence or 25–50 g (1–2 oz) sultanas or raisins.

4   Bring the pudding to the boil, lower the heat until the milk simmers steadily.

5   Fix the cover, bring to H/15 lb pressure on a medium heat and cook for 12 minutes. Allow pressure to drop at room temperature.

6   Spoon into a heatproof dish; you can brown under the grill.

TO VARY:

Cook sago, semolina and tapioca in the same way, but allow 7 minutes at H/15 lb pressure.

Gourmet Touch: **Rice Condé:** Let the rice pudding become cool, add a generous amount of whipped cream, spoon into a dish, top with well-drained canned or cooked fruit. Make a glaze by melting redcurrant jelly or sieved apricot jam with a little fruit syrup; cool. Spread over the fruit and top with more whipped cream.

CHOCOLATE SOUFFLÉ PUDDING

This is an interesting pudding because it separates during cooking. The top is like a very light sponge and the base is a custard-sauce mixture. Initial steaming unnecessary.

Serves 3–4
Pressure cooking time 5 mins

50 g (2 oz) butter or margarine
50 g (2 oz) caster sugar
2 large eggs

40 g (1½ oz) self-raising flour (or plain flour and ½ teaspoon baking powder)
1 tablespoon cocoa powder
12 tablespoons – 210 ml (7½ fl oz) milk

1   Cream the butter or margarine and sugar until soft and light.

2   Separate the egg yolks from the whites and beat the yolks into the creamed mixture.

3   Sieve the flour, or flour and baking powder, with the cocoa and fold into the mixture, then gradually beat in the milk. The mixture tends to curdle (separate) at this stage, but it does not spoil the mixture.

4   Whisk the egg whites until stiff, fold into the other ingredients.

5   Pour into a greased 18-cm (7-in) soufflé dish, cover well, see page 125.

6   Cook as the egg custard on page 134.

7   Serve hot or cold.

TO VARY:

Mocha Soufflé Pudding: Use moderately strong coffee in place of part or all of the milk; you may like to add an extra tablespoon sugar.

Lemon Soufflé Pudding: Grate the rind from 2 lemons; cream with the butter, etc. Squeeze out the juice and add enough water or milk to give 12 tablespoons; continue as in the basic pudding.
Other citrus fruits, i.e. oranges, grapefruit, etc., could be used.

Gourmet Touch: Cook the selected pudding, top with flaked almonds, a little sieved icing sugar, and brown under the grill.

Use half ground almonds and half flour (plus the baking powder) instead of all flour in the basic pudding.

COOKING CAKES UNDER PRESSURE

There are a number of good reasons for cooking cakes in a pressure cooker.

  a) To save fuel – you use the same amount of fuel in heating the oven to bake one cake as you do when filling the oven with food.

  b) To save time – the cooking period is a little shorter than when baking the cake.

  c) You may not have an oven due to restricted cooking equipment, either permanently or temporarily, as when on holiday caravanning or camping.

There is a small selection of cakes in this section, but these will give you an indication of just what can be achieved. It is a good idea to read pages 124-127, which give information on cooking puddings in the pressure cooker, as the same points apply.

FAMILY FRUIT CAKE

Serves 6–8
Steaming time 15 mins
Pressure cooking time 35 mins

---

170 g (6 oz) self-raising flour (or plain flour and 1½ level teaspoons baking powder)
110 g (4 oz) butter or margarine
110 g (4 oz) caster sugar
110 g (4 oz) dried fruit
50 g (2 oz) chopped candied peel
1 egg
Milk to mix

---

1   Sieve the flour, or flour and baking powder, into a mixing bowl.

2   Rub in the butter or margarine until the consistency of fine breadcrumbs, then add the sugar, fruit and peel.

3   Blend in the egg and enough milk to make a sticky consistency, i.e. until the mixture stands up in soft peaks, then spoon into a well-greased and floured 15-cm (6-in) cake tin; cover well.

4   Cook as stages 6–8 in the Chocolate Cake, below, but allow 35 minutes at L/5 lb pressure.

5   Dry out under a grill at low heat.

CHOCOLATE CAKE

Serves 6
Steaming time 15 mins
Pressure cooking time 25 mins

---

4 tablespoons milk
1 tablespoon golden syrup
25 g (1 oz) margarine
90 g (3½ oz) self-raising flour (or plain flour and 1 teaspoon baking powder)

½ teaspoon bicarbonate of soda
1 tablespoon cocoa
50 g (2 oz) caster sugar
Few drops vanilla essence

FOR THE TOPPING:
2–3 tablespoons icing sugar or
75 g (2 oz) plain chocolate and 15 g (½ oz) butter

---

1   Put the milk, golden syrup and margarine into a saucepan and heat until melted; do not allow to boil after this, otherwise the liquid evaporates.

2   Sieve the flour, or flour and baking powder, bicarbonate of soda and cocoa into a mixing bowl.

3   Add the sugar then the melted ingredients, and a few drops vanilla essence.

4   Beat the mixture thoroughly.

5   Pour into a well-greased and floured 15-cm (6-in) cake tin.

6   Cover thoroughly, stand on the trivet and add generous ¾ litre (1½ pt) boiling water.

7   Steam for 15 minutes then bring to L/5 lb pressure.

8   Cook for 25 minutes; allow pressure to drop. Turn the cake out of the tin, cool, and then top with sieved icing sugar or melted chocolate icing.

To melt chocolate: Break into small pieces, put into a basin with the butter. Heat over hot, but not boiling, water. Use as soon as the chocolate melts.

TO VARY:

Mocha Cake: use strong coffee in place of milk.

GINGERBREAD

Serves 6
Steaming time 15 mins
Pressure cooking time 25 mins

---

100 g (4 oz) self-raising flour (or plain flour and 1½ level teaspoons baking powder)
¾ level teaspoon bicarbonate of soda
½ teaspoon ground ginger

¼ teaspoon mixed spice
40 g (1½ oz) cooking fat or lard
25 g (1 oz) sugar
1½ level tablespoons golden syrup or treacle
4 tablespoons water
1 egg

1   Sieve all the dry ingredients together in a mixing bowl.

2   Melt the fat or lard, sugar and syrup or treacle in a pan.

3   Pour on to the dry ingredients and beat thoroughly.

4   Boil the water in the treacle pan so nothing is wasted, then beat into the cake mixture until bubbles appear on the surface.

5   Lastly add the egg and mix thoroughly.

6   Grease and flour a 15-cm (6-in) cake tin. Pour the mixture into the tin.

7   Cover thoroughly and cook as the chocolate cake, page 139.

TO VARY:

Lemon Gingerbread: Add the finely grated lemon zest (rind) of 1 lemon to the flour at stage 1. Use 2 tablespoons lemon juice in place of 2 tablespoons water at stage 4.

Gingerbread Pudding: Serve the cake hot, topped with apple purée, as a delicious dessert.

Sultana Gingerbread: Add 50 g (2 oz) sultanas at stage 3. They tend to sink in this soft mixture, but make a rather good topping if you turn the cake upside-down.

Gourmet Touch: **Almond Gingerbread:** Add 25 g (1 oz) ground almonds to the flour at stage 1. When the gingerbread is cooked and turned out of the tin, spread the top of the cake with a little apricot jam, then top with flaked almonds. This can also be served as a dessert with sliced, cooked apples.

TOPPINGS FOR CAKES

A pressure-cooked cake is soft on top, like a pudding, so 'dry out' under the grill set to a low heat, or dust with sugar or brush with a little warm honey or marmalade.

COOKING FRUIT

Fruit can be cooked under pressure, either as poached (often called stewed) fruit, or as a purée. Dried fruits become soft and plump, without the need to soak them. A great advantage of pressure cooking is that fruit can often be cooked in their own juice, without fear of burning in the pan.

Preparation: Peel and slice apples. To prevent discoloration either drop into a solution of 1 teaspoon kitchen salt to each ½ litre (1 pt) water, then rinse before cooking, or put immediately into the boiling syrup in the base of the cooker or cooking dish. Skin peaches by lowering gently into boiling water, leave for ½ minute, cool and remove the skin, then halve or slice. Halve and stone apricots, plums or other stoned fruit. If you prefer to cook these whole then prick once or twice with a fine fork or needle, so the syrup can penetrate.

FRUIT PURÉES

To make a smooth purée prepare the fruit as above, then cut into smaller pieces than for poaching. Make the syrup, as described on page 143, in the bottom of the pressure cooker, but allow to cool slightly if possible, as this helps the fruit to break down into a pulp. Add the fruit to the syrup. Never have the cooker more than half filled with fruit and syrup and allow a minimum of 280 ml (½ pt) syrup. Put the fruit into the syrup, there is no need to lower carefully, as when poaching fruit. Fix the cover, bring to H/15 lb pressure, lower the heat and cook as follows: soft fruits need 2–3 minutes, firmer fruits need 3–5 minutes. Reduce the pressure then spoon the pulp from the cooker. If desired, sieve or liquidise in the blender, although it is sufficiently smooth for most purposes. If the purée is a little liquid, strain off the syrup; this is delicious used in jellies. Fruit purées make good sauces over ice cream.

BURGUNDY PEARS

This is an excellent way of dealing with under-ripe or cooking pears; the timing given assumes they are moderately firm; if very hard, cook as below, reduce pressure, check whether tender and if necessary allow 2–3 minutes extra pressure cooking time.

Serves 4
Pressure cooking time 5 mins

---

4 large or 6 medium firm pears
1 orange
140 ml (¼ pt) red Burgundy

140 ml (¼ pt) water
1–2 tablespoons sugar
2 tablespoons redcurrant jelly

TO DECORATE:
few blanched almonds

---

1 Peel the pears, halve and core.

2 Pare thinly several strips of orange rind, squeeze out 1 tablespoon orange juice.

3 Put the pears into the cooker with the wine, water and orange rind and the 1 tablespoon orange juice.

4 Stir in the sugar, fix the cover, bring to H/15 lb pressure and cook for 5–6 minutes or until the pears are soft. Reduce pressure rapidly.

5 Lift the pears from the liquid and put into a serving dish.

6 Stir the jelly into the liquid in the pan; heat gently (without the cover) until dissolved. Taste the syrup, add more orange juice if desired. Strain over the pears.

7 Serve hot or cold, topped with almonds.

TO VARY:

Ginger Pears: Use 280 ml (½ pt) water (instead of wine and water) plus lemon juice and rind, and 50 g (2 oz) chopped preserved or crystallized ginger.

Pears in Cider: Use half cider and half water and flavour with a little apple jelly at stage 6.

Gourmet Touch: Cook pears but keep in the syrup. Remove orange rind, add 2–3 tablespoons brandy, at the end of stage 6, ignite, spoon into serving dish. Serve with ice cream.

TO POACH FRUIT

Soft fruits, such as blackcurrants, redcurrants, ripe gooseberries, rhubarb, loganberries and juicy apples, are better cooked, with sugar to taste, in a soufflé or similar dish in the cooker. You can add 2–3 tablespoons water if you like a lot of juice. Firmer fruits like hard apples, firm gooseberries, plums, apricots, peaches, pears, etc., are better if cooked in syrup, either in a dish, or the base of the cooker.

To make the syrup: boil 50–100 g (2–4 oz) sugar with each 280 ml

(½ pt) water. A strip of lemon or orange rind or a little lemon juice adds a pleasant flavour and helps to keep the fruit a good colour.

If using a dish: Place the dish with fruit and sugar, or syrup on the trivet. The cooker should contain 280 ml (½ pt) water.

If cooking in the base of the pan: Make a minimum of 280 ml (½ pt) syrup, lower the fruit into this. Never have the pressure cooker more than half filled with syrup and fruit. Fix the cover and bring to H/15 lb pressure. Lower the heat and cook as follows:

Soft fruits need 4 minutes; if slightly firm allow 5 minutes. Firmer fruits need 5 minutes, or 6 minutes if rather hard and under-ripe. Hard cooking pears need 7–8 minutes. Reduce the pressure under cold water, then remove the cover.

DRIED FRUIT

Wash the fruit well in hot water. Put into a basin and add boiling water. Allow a generous ½ litre (1 pt) water to each 450 g (1 lb) fruit.

Remove the trivet and pour the fruit and liquid into the cooker, add 2–3 tablespoons sugar and flavouring as desired, e.g. lemon rind, spice or 2–3 cloves. Bring to H/15 lb pressure and time as follows:

Apple rings: 6 minutes

Apricots: 3 minutes, use slightly less water, and lemon to flavour.

Peaches: 5 minutes

Prunes, pears, figs and fruit salad: 10 minutes

Allow pressure to drop at room temperature.

To give an interesting flavour to prunes, cook in well-strained weak tea instead or water. Figs have a richer flavour if cooked in well-strained weak coffee instead of water.

APPLE BROWN BETTY

Serves 4–6
Pressure cooking time 10 mins

---

450 g (1 lb) cooking apples
50 g (2 oz) butter or margarine
100 g (4 oz) breadcrumbs from a brown loaf
75 g (3 oz) dried fruit (currants, sultanas or raisins)
½–1 teaspoon mixed spice
75 g (3 oz) brown sugar

1–2 tablespoons golden syrup
1 tablespoon warm water

1 Peel and thinly slice the apples.

2 Grease a generous 1-kg (2-lb) pudding basin with half the butter or margarine.

3 Sprinkle a thin layer of the breadcrumbs round the inside of the basin.

4 Mix the rest of the crumbs with the dried fruit, spice and sugar.

5 Fill the basin with alternate layers of breadcrumb mixture and apples, beginning and ending with breadcrumbs.

6 Put the rest of the butter or margarine in tiny pieces on top of the pudding.

7 Mix the golden syrup with the warm water, pour over the ingredients in the basin.

8 Cover with greased greaseproof paper or foil, see page 125.

9 Stand the basin on the trivet, add ¾ litre (1½ pt) boiling water.

10 Fix the cover and bring steadily to H/15 lb pressure.

11 Lower the heat and cook for 10 minutes, then allow pressure to drop at room temperature.

12 Serve with cream or custard.

TO VARY:

Rhubarb Brown Betty: Use diced rhubarb in place of apples.

MAKING PRESERVES

Home-made jams, marmalades, chutneys are not only good to eat but they are also economical when made in a pressure cooker.

Usually one has to simmer the fruit, or the pulp, pips and peel, in the case of marmalade, slowly to extract the pectin (natural setting quality). This can be done with equal efficiency, but in far less time, in a pressure cooker.

When the fruits, or fruit and vegetables in the case of chutney, are tender, allow the pressure to drop, remove the cover and treat the pressure cooker as an ordinary preserving pan.

Always stir in the sugar over a low to medium heat then allow the preserve to boil rapidly, or steadily in the case of chutney, until setting point or the desired consistency is reached. Details for putting the preserves in jars and storing are given in the recipes.

Never have the cooker more than half filled when both fruit and liquid are added. If making a larger amount of marmalade use only half the water to soften the peel, then add the remainder with the sugar.

Trivet: This is not used in making preserves; only in bottling.

Pressure: Bring to M/10 lb pressure. If you only have H/15 lb, shorten time by at least 1 minute.

Reducing pressure: Allow to drop at room temperature.

Adding sugar, etc.: Warm the sugar if possible, add to the fruit and stir over a low heat in the open cooker until dissolved, then boil rapidly until setting point is reached.

Setting point: This is when the preserve reaches 104–105.5°C (220–222°F) for jelly, or if it forms a skin and wrinkles when cooled on a saucer, or hangs in a flake when cooled on a wooden spoon.

Potting: Put into hot jars; marmalade or whole fruit jams should cool slightly in the cooker, then stir to distribute the peel or fruit. Cover with waxed circles and final cover and store in a cool dry place.

PROPORTIONS FOR PRESERVES

Soft fruits, such as strawberries and raspberries, have not been included since they take such a short time to cook in a pan. Out of each 450 g (1lb) sugar you should have about 710 g (1⅔lb) preserve. Metric measures ae given accurately for hams as it is important.

JAMS					
FRUIT	TO PREPARE	WATER	SUGAR	LEMON JUICE	MINUTES AT M/10 LB
450 g (1 lb) when prepared {Apple (450 g/1 lb) Blackberry (450 g/1 lb)	see page 142	140 ml (¼pt)	900 g (2 lb)	-	7
Apricots-fresh or plums or greengages-dried	see page 142 Add kernels if wished see page 142	140 ml (¼ pt) scant ¾ l (1½pt)	450 g (1 lb) 1.35 kg (3 lb)	1 tablespoon 3 tablespoons	4 10 at H/15 lb
Blackcurrants	see page 142	420 ml (¾pt)	675 g (1½lb)	_	3-4
Damsons	see page 142	140 ml (¼ pt)	550 g (1 lb 4 oz)	_	5
Gooseberries	see page 142	140 ml (¼ pt)	450 g (1 lb) if ripe; 550 g (1 lb 4 oz) if very green	_	4-5
MARMALADE					
Lemon	see page 148	generous ½ l (1 pt)	½kg (2 lb)	_	8
Grapefruit	see page 148	very generous ½ l (1¼pt)	scant 1¼kg (2½lb)	2 tablespoons	10
Seville Orange -bitter -sweeter	see page 148 see page 148	generous ½ l (1 pt) ¾ l (1½pt)	½kg (2 lb) 1½kg (3 lb)	_ 2 tablespoons	10 10

JELLIES

To prepare the fruit add 280ml (½ pt) water to each 450g (1lb) fruit, then continue as page 148.

Apples and blackcurrants should be cooked for 5 minutes at M/10 lb pressure; crab apples for 8 minutes at M/10lb; redcurrants for only 1 minute. To each generous ½ l (1pt) liquid allow 450g (1lb) sugar.

PERFECT JAMS

1 Choose fruits that are ripe, but not over-ripe, and free from blemishes. Prepare as for cooking.

2 Put the fruit with water (see table page 147) into the base of the cooker.

3 Fix the cover, bring to M/10 lb pressure and cook as given in the table on page 147; allow pressure to drop.

4 Remove the cover.

5 Add the sugar with lemon juice if necessary. Stir in the open cooker until the sugar has dissolved.

6 Boil rapidly until setting point is reached.

7 Spoon into hot jars and seal.

PERFECT JELLIES

Some fruits – apples, damsons, blackcurrants, redcurrants, etc., – are ideal for a jelly. The process is as follows:

1 Wash the fruit, there is no need to peel or remove stones, etc.

2 Follow directions for jam, stages 2–4 above.

3 Put the fruit pulp through a jelly bag or several thicknesses of muslin.

4 Measure the liquid and add 450 g (1 lb) sugar to each 560 ml (1 pt) liquid.

5 Return the liquid to the pan; continue as in stages 6 and 7 above.

YOUR OWN RECIPES

If a particular jam, marmalade or jelly is not given here, you can adapt your own recipe. Use only half the usual amount of water, as there is less evaporation when cooking under pressure. Find a similar fruit and use this as in stages 6 and 7 above.

FREEZING THE FRUITS

Freeze the prepared fruit to make jam or marmalade when required. Use double the amount of lemon juice to compensate for loss of pectin.

PERFECT MARMALADE

It is essential that the peel of the fruit is softened before adding the sugar; it never softens *after* this. A good test is to see if you can rub it between your forefinger and thumb after pressure cooking.

1   Wash the fruit well; halve, squeeze out all the juice. Remove pips and pith, tie loosely in a muslin bag.

2   Cut the peel into quarters.

3   Put the fruit and the bag of pips, etc., into the cooker with half or all the water (see comments on liquid, page 146).

4   Bring to M/10 lb pressure, time as in the table on page 147.

5   Allow pressure to drop, and then remove the cover.

6   Lift out the bag of pips, and squeeze over the contents of the cooker, for these provide much of the pectin.

7   Lift out the peel and when cool enough to handle, chop or slice as thinly as desired.

8   Stir in the warmed sugar, plus lemon juice if required, then boil rapidly until setting point is reached. Test early for marmalade (see page 146), as the setting period can be missed.

9   Cool slightly, stir, and then put into warm jars and cover.

BOTTLING FRUIT

It is wise to preserve fruit for use during the winter months. Even if you have a freezer, you will find that certain fruits, such as peaches, pears and tomatoes have a better flavour when bottled.

1   Prepare the fruit as though for cooking or serving. It is advisable to prick apricots, peaches and similar fruit if leaving whole, as this allows the syrup to penetrate.

  Put peaches and tomatoes into boiling water for ½ minute then remove the skins.

2   Make a syrup of sugar and water as though poaching fruit (see page 143), keep this boiling.

3   Warm the bottling jars inside with hot water, tip this out then stand the jars in a bowl of boiling water; also cover the lids of the jars with boiling water.

4   Pack the jars with the fruit, push down firmly, do not bruise; leave standing in the boiling water while you do this.

5   Cover the fruit and fill the jars *almost* to the top with the boiling syrup (use brine for tomatoes). You must leave a little space, so the syrup will not boil out during bottling; shake the jars as you fill them to get rid of air bubbles.

6   Wipe the necks of the jars, put on the lids, clip or screw in position; give screw bands a quarter turn back to allow for expansion.

7   Meanwhile have the cooker, with the trivet in position (rim side

uppermost), filled with ¾ litre (1½ pt) boiling water.

8 Lift the jars of fruit straight from the boiling water in the bowl to the boiling water in the pressure cooker. Make sure the jars do not touch each other, or the sides or top of the cooker.

9 Bring to L/5 lb pressure *steadily*. Time the bottling process: Allow 1 minute for all fruits *except* grapefruit, peaches, pears, pineapples, quinces and strawberries which require 3 minutes; garden rhubarb needs 2 minutes; whole tomatoes need 5 minutes.

10 Allow the pressure to drop at room temperature; if you move the cooker off the heat do this gently, so the jars do not shake.

11 Remove the jars from the cooker, tighten screw bands.

12 Test to see the lids have sealed after 24 hours.

13 It is wise to oil the inside of screw bands before storing the fruit, to stop them from rusting.

FREEZING AND BOTTLING VEGETABLES

When bottling or freezing vegetables it is ESSENTIAL to blanch them first. This means they must be subjected to a certain amount of heat, either in boiling water or in the pressure cooker (which is quicker and easier). It is now possible to buy a blanching basket to fit into the pressure cooker.

The blanching process destroys harmful bacteria and ensures that both the colour and texture and flavour of the vegetables are retained. After blanching, follow directions for freezing as given in your maker's instruction book.

The times for blanching in boiling water OR in the pressure cooker are given on pages 151-152, together with an indication as to which vegetables can be frozen with success and which can be bottled, so you can make your own choice. After blanching, plunge the vegetables into ice-cold water to prevent their becoming over-soft.

Brine: Vegetables are bottled in brine. To prepare this: Add 25 g (1 oz) kitchen salt to each generous 1 litre (2 pt) water. Boil before using. It is possible to colour the brine with green colouring to use with peas, beans, etc.

Process of bottling: Prepare and wash the vegetables as for cooking, blanch as on pages 151-152, then cool. Follow the directions for fruit bottling, except that it is essential to use M/10 lb pressure for the time given in the table on pages 151-152.

VEGETABLE	PREPARATION	BLANCHING		BOTTLING	FOR FREEZING
		Minutes in boiling water	Minutes at M/10lb pressure	Minutes at M/10lb pressure	
Artichoke - *Jerusalem* *Globe*	Scrape, keep white, as page 111 As for cooking	5 7-10	1...T 1...T	35	Fairly good
Asparagus	Trim stalks, cut into even lengths	2-4	To M/10 lb[+]	30-35	Good
Aubergine	Peel, slice	4	1...T	35	Good
Beans - *Broad* (young)	Choose Green Windsor, Triple White	3	To M/10lb[+]	40	Good
French (young)	String, keep whole	3	To M/10lb[+]	40	Good
Runner (young)	String and slice (fairly thickly for freezing)	3	To M/10lb[+]	40	Good
Beetroot	Scald, rub off skins, see special note	15-20	15-20	40	Fair
Broccoli	Trim to give tight heads	3	To M/10lb[+]	-	Very good
Brussels sprouts	Remove outer leaves	2-3	1-2	-	Good
Carrots	Scrape, leave whole if young; dice or slice if older	5-10	2-6	40	Good
Cauliflower	Divide into flowerets	3	1...T	-	Fairly good
Celeriac	Peel, dice, cook	-	-	-	Fairly good
Celery - *hearts* *outer*	Divide -	6 _	1...T 5...T	35 35	Fair Fair
Chicory	Whole head	4	1...T	_	Fair
Corn on the Cob	Remove leaves	4-6	2-2½	45	Very good
Courgettes	Slice	1	1...T	_	Good
Macédoine vegetables	As individual root vegetables, peas and beans	Max. time	Max. time	Max. time	Good

Mushrooms	See special note	–	–	35-40	Very good
Peas	Remove from pod. Onward, Laxton Lincoln recommended	2	1	35	Good
Peppers	See special note	–	–	40	Very good
Potatoes - *new* *old*	Scrape, use small Peel and dice	5 –	2 4 at H/15 lb	45 45	Fair Fair
Spinach	Wash – blanch only 225 g (8 oz) at a time	1	To M/10lb+	–	Very good
Sweetcorn	Name given when kernels removed from cob	3	1+++ (see special note)	45	Good
Turnips, parsnips, swedes	Diced	3-5	1-2	45	Fairly good

T – means you need the trivet.
+ Simply bring up to pressure then allow this to drop.
+++ Remove leaves, strip the kernels from the cob.
Beetroot: Use only young small beetroot.
Mushrooms: Skin and pre-cook until liquid flows, pack in own liquid.
Peppers: Skin, if wished, by leaving in hot oven for 6-8 minutes, pull off skins. Slice, remove cores and seeds, pack in layers, no liquid needed.

MAKING CHUTNEY

Home-made chutney is delicious, and quickly and easily made in the pressure cooker.

There are certain important points:

Do not use a smaller quantity of sugar and vinegar, for the chutney will not keep if you do. Always use pure malt vinegar. Cook the vegetables, fruit, etc., at H/15 lb pressure, reduce the pressure then use the open cooker just as you would an ordinary preserving pan.

Stir until the sugar has thoroughly dissolved to eliminate any possibility of its burning, then boil steadily, not rapidly as when jam-making, until the desired consistency is obtained.

Take particular care when covering chutney or any other preserve containing vinegar, for vinegar can cause rusting on the inside of the metal cover. Use a waxed circle, then several thicknesses of brown paper or a round of cardboard under the metal cover. Cover chutney thoroughly and store in a cool dry place.

Gourmet Touch: **Pickled Fruits:** You can bottle fruits in a sweetened vinegar, rather than an ordinary syrup. Follow the directions for bottling fruit, page 149. The vinegar syrup can be flavoured with spice, ground ginger or cinnamon. The most suitable fruits are pears, crab apples (bottle whole) and peaches. They are delicious with cold meats.

GREEN TOMATO AND APPLE CHUTNEY

Makes nearly 2 kg (4 lb)
Pressure cooking time 10 mins

---

340 g (12 oz) onions
450 g (1 lb) cooking apples (weight after peeling)
450 g (1 lb) green tomatoes
280 ml (½ pt) brown or white malt vinegar
½–1 teaspoon salt
1–2 teaspoons mixed pickling spice
340 g (12 oz) sugar, white (loaf, preserving or granulated) or brown (Demerara or moist brown)
170–225 g (6–8 oz) sultanas

---

1 Peel the onions and apples, skin the tomatoes.

2 Chop the vegetables and fruit and put into the pressure cooker.

3 Add the vinegar, the salt, and the pickling spice tied securely in muslin.

4 Fix the cover and bring to H/15 lb pressure.

5 Cook for 10 minutes, and then cool under cold water.

6 Remove the cover, add the sugar and dried fruit and stir over a low heat until the sugar has dissolved; remove the bag of spice.

7 Boil steadily in the open pan until the consistency of a thick purée, stir from time to time.

8 Spoon into hot jars and cover.

TO VARY:

Apple and Ginger: Use 1 kg (2 lb) prepared apples, omit tomatoes; add 1–2 teaspoons ground ginger plus 100 g (4 oz) chopped preserved ginger with the sugar.

Gooseberry and Mint: Use gooseberries in place of tomatoes, and add 4–6 tablespoons chopped fresh mint leaves when the chutney is cooked, i.e. stage 7.

Green Tomato: Use 750 g (1½ lb) green tomatoes and 225 g (8 oz) prepared apples; proceed as above but add 2–3 crushed cloves garlic at stage 2.

Gourmet Touch: **Apricot and Almond:** Use fresh apricots in place of tomatoes. Add 1–2 level teaspoons almond essence to the vinegar and 100–150 g (4–6 oz) coarsely chopped blanched almonds when the chutney is cooked at stage 6.

MAKING KETCHUPS

1   The basic rules about vinegar, sugar, etc., as given for chutney are just as important for ketchups.

2   If you have a liquidizer and do not mind tiny particles of skin and pips in the sauce, use it instead of the sieve.

3   If you sieve the ingredients, then make certain you rub all the pulp through the sieve, otherwise the sauce will not be as thick as it should.

4   Seal containers of sauces very well (read comments on covering, page 152).

5   Store for 2–3 weeks before using. Ketchups keep for about 1 year.

TOMATO KETCHUP

Makes generous 1 litre (2 pt)
Pressure cooking time 10 mins

---

280 ml (½ pt) white malt vinegar
2 teaspoons mixed pickling spice
Scant 2 kg (4 lb) tomatoes
1 medium onion
450 g (1 lb) apples
125 g (5 oz) sugar, preferably white
1 teaspoon salt
Shake cayenne pepper
Shake black pepper

---

1   Simmer the vinegar and pickling spice in the cooker for 10 minutes. Do not bring to pressure but lay the cover over the top of the

cooker; strain the vinegar.

2   Cut up the tomatoes, do not skin as this improves the colour of the ketchup; peel and chop the onion and apples.

3   Put the fruit and vegetables into the pressure cooker with the vinegar. Fix the cover and bring to H/15 lb pressure.

4   Lower the heat and cook for 10 minutes. Reduce pressure under cold water.

5   Remove the cover and sieve or liquidise the mixture.

6   Return to the open pan with the sugar, salt and peppers.

7   Stir over a low heat until the sugar has dissolved, then boil steadily until a thick coating consistency is obtained.

8   Pour into hot jars or bottles and seal.

MUSTARD PICKLES

Makes about 1½ kg (3 lb)
Pressure cooking time 1 min

---

1 kg (2 lb) vegetables (see below)
Brine (see stage 2)
420 ml (¾ pt) malt vinegar
1–2 teaspoons pickling spice
1–2 teaspoons ground ginger
1 tablespoon flour or ½ tablespoon cornflour
½ tablespoon turmeric powder
½–1 tablespoon mustard powder
50 g (2 oz) sugar

---

1   Prepare the vegetables; these can be cauliflower, marrow, onion, cucumber, small green tomatoes, and runner beans. Cut them into even sizes.

2   Make a brine: allow 50 g (2 oz) kitchen salt to each generous ½ litre (1 pt) water; do not heat. Put the vegetables in this and leave for 12 hours. Keep well-covered with a plate on top.

3   The next day, strain and rinse well under running cold water, drain.

4   Bring the 420 ml (¾ pt) malt vinegar and 1–2 teaspoons pickling spice just to boiling point, strain the vinegar.

5 Put the vegetables into the cooker with 280 ml (½ pt) of the spiced vinegar, and the ground ginger.

6 Fix the cover, bring to H/15 lb pressure, and cook for 1 minute only, so the vegetables do not become too soft. Reduce the pressure.

7 Blend the flour or cornflour, turmeric and mustard powder with the remaining vinegar, stir into the vegetable mixture, add the sugar and continue stirring until thickened.

8 Put into jars, cover and seal as described under chutney (page 152).

INDEX

A

Adzuki bean soup 39
Almond custard 135
Almond gingerbread 141
Almond pudding 136
Anchovy sauce 53
Apple and ginger chutney 153
Apple Brown Betty 144
Apple sauce 105
Apple soup 48
Apricot and almond chutney 154
Artichoke cream 32
Artichoke soup 31
Artichokes, globe 111
Artichokes, Jerusalem 111
Asparagus 111
Aubergines 111

B

Bacon and cabbage chowder 42
Barley 123
Beans, broad 111
    French 112
    runner 112
Béchamel sauce 53
Beef consommé 27
Beef galantine 94
Beef olives 76
Beetroot 112
Blackbean soup 39
Blackcap pudding 131
Blanquette of chicken 78
Blanquette of guinea fowl 78
Blanquette of rabbit 78
Blanquette of veal 77
Boiled bacon 89
Boiled chicken 91
Boiled ham 89
Boiled lamb with caper sauce 92
Boiled salt beef 89
Boiled salt beef and dumplings 90
Bolognese sauce 104
Bortsch 29
Bortsch with cooked beetroot 30
Bottling fruit 149
Bottling vegetables 150-152
Bouquet garni 16
Braised beef 87
Braised chicken 88
Braised heart 84
Braised lambs' kidneys 87
Braised liver 85
Braised liver Lyonnaise 86
Braised liver Niçoise 86
Braised ox kidney 86
Braised oxtail 88
Braised pheasants 87
Braised pigeons 86
Braised sweetbreads 87
Braised vegetables 84
Brandy butter 128
Brawn 93
Bread and butter pudding 134
Bread sauce 107
Brine 150
Broccoli 112
Brown stock 25
Burgundy pears 142
Butter bean soup 38

C

Cabbage 112
Canned puddings 132
Cannellini bean soup 39
Caper sauce 53, 92
Carrot soup 32
Carrots 112
Carrots Vichy 112
Castle puddings 133
Cauliflower 113
Celeriac soup 32
Celery 113
Celery and almond soup 32
Celery soup 32
Chaudfroid of chicken 92
Cheese sauce 53
Cherry plum soup 49
Chestnut soup 49
Chicken and lemon brawn 94
Chicken broth 46
Chicken Chasseur 80
Chicken consommé 28
Chicken fricassée 122

Chicken galantine 95
Chicken purée soup 42
Chicken soups 42
Chicken Supreme 92
Chicken Velouté 92
Chicory 113
Chilli con carne 73
Chocolate cake 139
Chocolate chip pudding 132
Chocolate crème 135
Chocolate crumb pudding 136
Chocolate custard 135
Chocolate pudding 132
Chocolate sauce 132
Chocolate soufflé pudding 133
Christmas pudding 128-130
Chutney 152-154
Cod and tomato savoury 54
Cod en cocotte 56
Cod Flamande 62
Cod Jamaican 55
Cod's roe 63
Coffee custard 135
Coffee pudding 132
Coffee walnut cream 135
Cold bortsch 30
Consommé Indienne 28
Consommé Jardinière 29
Consommé Julienne 29
Coq au vin 81
Corn on the cob 115, 151
Cornish pudding 100
Courgettes 113, 151
Court-bouillon 54

Cranberry sauce 105
Cream of chicken soup 42
Cream of kidney soup 45
Cream of tomato soup 37
Cream of vegetable soup 34
Creamed curried fish 60
Creamed mince 73
Creamed smoked haddock 59
Creamed tripe and onions 82
Creamy pumpkin soup 36
Crème à la Grecque 21
Crème brûlée 136
Croutons 25
Cumberland sauce 102
Curried fish 59
Curried mince 73
Curried rice 120
Curries 108

D
Danish chicken soup 28
Devilled fish 60
Devilled herring 61
Devilled kidney soup 45
Dhal 118
Dill sauce 53
Dried fruit 144
Dried pea soup 40
Dried vegetables 116-117
Dumplings, savoury 100

E
Economical Christmas pudding 128
Economical sponge pudding 132
Egg and cheese stuffing 64
Egg custard 134
Espagnole sauce 103

F
Family fruit cake 139
Family liver pâté 19
Fennel sauce 53
Fish cakes 64
Fish casserole 60
Fish chowder 41
Fish mousse 65
Fish stock 26
Fish with anchovy butter 56
Flavoured butters 56
Flavourings (joints) 98
(rice) 120
Flemish stew 72
Florentine turbot 55
Freezing vegetables 150
Fresh pea soup 41
Fruit puddings 127
Fruit purées 142

G
German carrot soup 33
Giblet stuffing 102
Ginger pears 143
Ginger pudding 132
Gingerbread 140
Gingerbread pudding 141
Glazed bacon 89
Glazed salt beef 90
Golden Christmas pudding 130

Golden dumplings 101
Golden pudding 132
Gooseberry and mint chutney 153
Goulash 75
Gravy 96
Green tomato and apple chutney 153
Green tomato chutney 154
Green Vichyssoise 34
Ground nut soup 50

H
Haddock Duglère 62
Hake Maltesa 62
Hake Portugaise 56
Ham stock 26
Haricot bean soup 40
Herb dumplings 101
Herbed chicken 107
Herbed lamb 108
Herbed mutton 108
Herring roes 63
Hollandaise sauce 107
Horseradish dumplings 101
Horseradish sauce 108

I
Iced consommé 28
Iced tomato soup 37
Irish stew 74

J
Jams 147-148
Jellied consommé 28
Jellied bortsch 30
Jellied tomato consommé 28
Jellies 147-148
Jugged hare 79
Jugged rabbit 79

K
Kedgeree 107
Kentish chicken pudding 100
Kidney soup 44
Kipper pâté 19
Kippers 59

L
Lambs' tongues 91
Lancashire hotpot 74
Leeks 114
Lemon custard 135
Lemon gingerbread 141
Lemon rice 121
Lemon sauce 133
Lemon soufflé pudding 138
Lentil dhal 118
Lentil soup 38
Luxury pâté 21

M
Macaroni cheese 123
Macaroon apricot custard 135
Mackerel with gooseberry sauce 57
Madeira sauce 104
Marmalade 147, 148
Marrow 114
Milk puddings 136
Minestrone soup 47
Mint sauce 108
Mocha cake 140
Mocha soufflé pudding 138
Mock braised duckling 85
Mulligatawny soup 46
Mushroom and tomato stuffing 64
Mushroom sauce 53

Mushroom stuffing 64
Mustard dumplings 101
Mustard pickles 155
Mustard sauce 55

O
One-stage sponge mixture 132
Onion and celery soup 35
Onion cream soup 35
Onion dumplings 101
Onion sauce 108
Onion soup 34
Onions 114
Orange custard 135
Orange sauce 103
Ox tongue 90

P
Parsley and lemon stuffing 102
Parsley sauce 53
Parsnips 114
Pasta, to boil 122
Pears in cider 143
Peas 114
Pepper sauce 104
Peppers 114
Pickled fruits 153
Plain sponge pudding 131
Pois à la Française 114
Pollo alla cacciatore 81
Porridge 123
Pot roast 96
Potato and carrot soup 32
Potato soup 32
Potatoes 115
Poulet à la Marengo 82

Poultry stock 26
Prawn stuffing 64
Pulses 116-117
Pumpkin Soup 35
Pumpkin and sesame
  soup 36

R
Rabbit pudding 100
Ragoût of oxtail 79
Ragoût of venison 78
Rhubarb Brown
  Betty 145
Rice condé 137
Rice pudding 136
Rice stuffing 102
Rice, to boil 120
Rillettes 22
Risotto 121
Risotto alla
  Finanziera 122
Risotto alla Milanese
  121

S
Saffron lamb 74
Saffron rice 121
Sage and onion
  stuffing 101
Salmon à la
  Condorcet 66
Salmon mousse 65
Salmon pâté 21
Salsify 113
Savoury beef 108
Savoury mince 73
Savoury rice 121
Scotch broth 45
Seafood pâté 21
Seakale 113
Shellfish 59
Shellfish chowder 42
Skate fines herbes 58
Smoked fish 59
Smoked haddock 59
Sole au gratin 56
Sole Jamaican 55

Sole Meunière 57
Sole Mexicaine 62
Sole Mornay 56
Sole Véronique 62
Soupe à l'oignon
  gratinée 35
Soused fish 61
Soused herring 61
Soused mackerel 61
Spaghetti alla
  Bolognese 123
Spaghetti alla
  Milanese 123
Spare ribs 75
Spinach 115
Sponge puddings 130
Spring greens 115
Sprouts, Brussels 115
Steak and kidney 71
Steak and kidney pie
  71
Steak and kidney
  pudding 98
Steamed roes 63
Stewed steak 70
Stocks 25-27
Stuffed fillets of sole
  63
Suet puddings 127
Sultana gingerbread
  141
Swedes 115
Sweet and sour spare
  ribs 75
Sweet rice 121
Sweetcorn 115

T
Tajine Tfaia 75
Taramasalata 20
Terrine of chicken 95
Terrine of game 95
Tomato and rice soup
  37
Tomato consommé
  28
Tomato ketchup 154

Tomato sauce 105
Tomato soup 36
Tomatoes 115
Tongue in Madeira
  sauce 91
Tongue in walnut
  mayonnaise 91
Tripe au gratin 83
Tripe Niçoise 83
Tripe rolls 83
Trout amandine 58
Trout mousse 65
Turbot Hollandaise
  107
Turbot in cream 56
Turbot Niçoise 58
Turkey and tarragon
  soup 43
Turkey soups 43
Turnips 115

V
Veal birds 77
Veal Marengo 72
Veal stuffing 102
Vegetable pudding
  100
Vegetable soup 33
Vegetable stock 26
Velouté sauce 53
Vichyssoise soup 34
Viennoise pudding
  135

W
Wellington casserole
  72
White sauce 53
White stock 26
Wine sauce 53